The Art of the Kariye Camii

ARCHAEOLOGY AND ART PUBLICATIONS

SCALA

The Art of the Kariye Camii

Robert Ousterhout

Scala Publishers Ltd
in association with
Archaeology and Art Publications

Copyright text: © Robert Ousterhout, 2002

First published in 2002 by
Scala Publishers Ltd
Gloucester Mansions
140a Shaftesbury Avenue
London WC2H 8HD

In association with
Archaeology and Art Publications
Hayriye Cad. Çorlu Apt. 3/4
80060 Galatasaray
Istanbul

❖ Prepared with the assistance and support
of the Turkish Ministry of Culture

ISBN 1 85759 249 2
ISBN 975-6899-76-x

Series Editors: Brian Johnson and Nezih Başgelen
Pubication research: Archaeology and Art Publications

Edited by Helena Drysdale
Designed by Anikst Design
Printed and bound in Turkey by Ofset Yapımevi

TITLE PAGE ILLUSTRATION: Detail from the *Deesis* mosaic
(see page 28)
FRONTISPIECE: Detail from the *Koimesis* (see page 22)

PHOTOGRAPHIC CREDITS
The photographs on the pages listed below, are credited to the
following sources:

© Robert Ousterhout:
pages 48, 90, 91 (*below right*), 92–93 and 106

© Archaeology and Art Publications:
pages 10–11, 13, 18, 20, 22, 30–31, 32–34, 36–37, 38, 40–41,
42–47, 50–57, 59, 60–69, 71–72, 74–75, 76–7, 79, 80, 84–7, p.
95–96), 97 (*left*), 98, 101–102, 105, 109, 112, 115–17 and 123
(*left*) (phot. Gültekin Tetik)

pages 2–3, 6, 24–25, 26–9, 39, 82–3, 113, 118 and 123 (*right*)
(phot. Nezih Başgelen)

pages 16 and 91 (*top*) (Paspates)

page 91 (*below right*) (Lenoir)

© E.J.W. Hawkins, courtesy of the Courtauld Institute, London:
pages 14 and 97 (*above and below right*)

© Dumbarton Oaks:
pages 15, 73 and 81

Courtesy of Çelik Gülersoy:
page 89

NOTE: Location numbers given in the plan on page 9 appear in
bold throughout the text.

CONTENTS

PREFACE

This is an introduction to one of Istanbul's major sites, once the famed Chora Monastery from the Byzantine period, subsequently converted to the Kariye Camii, and presently the Kariye Museum.* The first chapters of the book outline the building's history and its spectacular mosaic and fresco decoration. Later chapters go into greater detail and suggest several different ways of looking at both building and decoration.

The complex and occasionally confusing plan of the building is organized as follows:

The *naos* was the main worship space, in the center of the building and covered by a dome on pendentives (spherical triangles that make the transition from arches to dome). The eastern extension of the naos is the *bema* or sanctuary, where the altar was located, directly in front of the apse. It was originally separated from the main part of the naos by a marble screen. The naos preserves some mosaic decoration, marble revetments, and sculpture.

To each side of the bema were side chapels called *pastophoria*, with the *prothesis* to the north, where the Eucharist was prepared, and the *diakonikon* to the south, which was a vestry. By the fourteenth century, the diakonikon functioned as a private chapel. Both preserve fresco fragments.

The two-storied *north annex* adjoined the naos. Its lower level *passageway* may have been a vestry, with traces of simple frescoes preserved. Its upper level was possibly the founder's *study*, housing the monastic library, with a window overlooking the naos.

To the west were two broad *narthexes*, or entry vestibules, decorated with mosaics. The inner narthex is also called the *esonarthex*. The outer narthex, or *exonarthex*, was opened by an arcaded portico façade and originally had a *belfry* at the southwest corner. The narthexes preserve mosaics, marble revetments, and sculpture.

Along the south side was the *parekklesion*, or subsidiary chapel, which functioned as a funeral chapel. Its frescoes are almost entirely preserved.

Between the parekklesion and the naos is a small, frescoed *passageway* connecting to two small rooms, an unfinished *storeroom* and an *oratory*, possibly a monk's cell. The latter is undecorated but has a window overlooking the naos.

A lavishly decorated Byzantine church like the Chora could be "read" on many levels. For the simple monk living in the monastery during Byzantine times, or for today's uninitiated tourist, its decoration presents illustrations from the holy books—subjects occasionally familiar, occasionally obscure.

On another level, the decoration resonates with the Byzantine liturgy, and the art of the Chora reflects the rituals that marked the daily life of a Byzantine monastic church. On yet another level, the art of the Chora reflects the patronage of one of Byzantium's greatest intellectuals; it is as sophisticated and erudite as a contemporary work of Byzantine literature, structured like a vast epic poem.

---

*Cami is the Turkish word for mosque. C is pronounced J in Turkish, so the building's name is pronounced KAH-ree-yay JAH-mee. Sometimes the word *cami* is spelled *djami*, following the French, but it is pronounced the same.

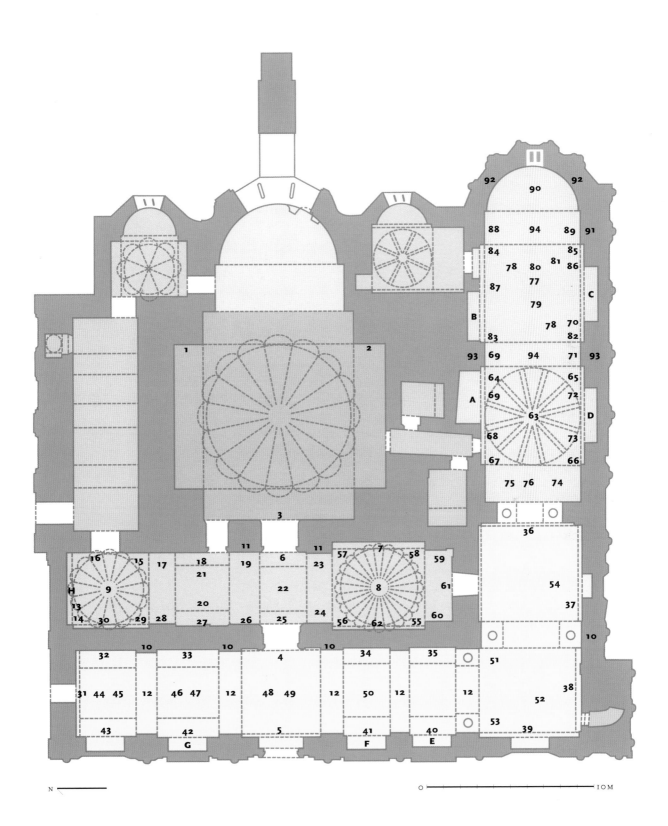

A general view of the Kariye Camii from the southeast, showing the apses of the parekklesion and naos. Both are decorated with niches and patterned brick, and the naos apse is braced by a flying buttress.

The Kariye Camii was originally the main church of the Chora Monastery, one of the oldest and most important religious foundations of Byzantine Constantinople. Located by the Adrianople Gate (Edirne Kapı), the Chora lay outside the city wall that Emperor Constantine I had constructed when he refounded the city in the fourth century; the site was only barely enclosed by the Land Wall of Theodosius II in the early fifth century. Although inside the Theodosian Wall, during Byzantine times this area remained rural. This may explain the appellation *chora* (Χωρα), which in Greek translates as "land," "country," or "in the country"—like English extramural religious foundations designated "in the fields" or Roman churches "fuori le mura." The word chora also has other meanings, and, as we shall see, was reinterpreted here in a mystical sense.

Although the site was allegedly consecrated for Christian use by the burial of the relics of St. Babylas and his disciples at the beginning of the fourth century—before the refounding of the city by Constantine the Great—nothing from this period survives. The earliest archaeological evidence dates from the sixth century. This coincides with the life of a certain St. Theodore, supposedly an uncle of Empress Theodora, who was said to have founded a monastery here that was subsequently destroyed in an earthquake and rebuilt by the Emperor Justinian.

The east façade, viewed from the garden, best reveals the Kariye's history. Below the main apse, remains of substructures are visible. The large arches may date from the sixth century; they were filled in during the ninth century. All that can be surmised from the substructures is that they created a platform on the sloping ground for the construction of a building, of which nothing survives. The present naos, the main space for worship in the building, dates from two phases from the Komnenian period, one in the late eleventh century, the other in the early twelfth. The present apse belongs to the early twelfth-century phase.

Archaeologists in the 1950s were surprised to find two phases of construction so close in date. The east part of the building suggests a reason. The Chora was built on unstable ground that continues to shift downhill. A crack about four cms (1 ½ inches) wide runs through the eastern part of the building. Though carefully patched, it breaks through the vaulting of the sanctuary and disfigures the frescoes in the parekklesion. It seems likely that the eleventh-century church collapsed, perhaps following an earthquake, and was reconstructed with a more stable design in the early twelfth century. The problems persisted, however, and the flying buttress was added in the fourteenth century to stabilize the apse. Borrowed from the French Gothic, the flying buttress is unusual in Byzantine architecture and was not fully understood. As the unstable ground continued to shift, the buttress actually moved away from the building and one of its flyers collapsed. When it was restored in the 1950s, it was partially supported by scaffolding. Today the flying buttress gives no more than the appearance of support.

The next place to examine the history is inside the naos. The positions of its north, west, and south walls were determined in the eleventh century. Byzantine writers attribute this phase of the building to Maria Doukaina, mother-in-law of Emperor Alexios I Komnenos. It can thus be dated ca. 1077–81. Evidence of a narrower apse flanked by lateral apses was found in the sanctuary excavations of 1957–58. This, combined with the fixed positions of the other walls, suggests the most likely reconstruction of Maria's church as a cross-in-square type, with a small dome raised above four columns. This was the most common Byzantine church type during the ninth through fourteenth centuries.

The Chora's plan was altered in the rebuilding of the early twelfth century, when the columns were replaced with sturdy corner piers supporting broad arches and a considerably larger dome. The naos opens eastward into a broad bema, which replaced the earlier narrow apse. This design is sometimes called an "atrophied Greek-cross plan"—that of a cross with equal and relatively short arms. This was deemed more stable than its predecessor, and it created a more spacious interior. This period of reconstruction can be attributed to the Sebastokrator (crown prince) Isaak Komnenos and dated to the 1120s. Isaak, who is pictured in the Deesis mosaic in the inner narthex, was nephew of Maria and brother of Emperor John II Komnenos, who was responsible for the construction of the contemporary Pantokrator monastery (Zeyrek Camii). Isaak had a tomb prepared for himself at the Chora, though he later had it moved to the Kosmosoteira monastery at Pherrai, in Greek Thrace, where he was buried.

Although located at the city's edge, the Chora gained importance in the last Byzantine centuries because of its proximity to the main imperial residence at the Blachernae Palace, the meager remains of which lie further north, towards the Golden Horn.

The Chora seems to have suffered during the Latin Occupation of Constantinople (1204–61), after which we hear complaints about its upkeep. The scholar Maximos Planudes complained about the deterioration of the monastic library, which apparently precipitated his departure from the Chora around 1300. The Patriarch Athanasios, who stayed at the Chora when visiting the emperor at the Blachernae Palace, complained in a letter written around 1305, "I have at least twenty followers who have no place to sleep and are freezing and covered with mud. If my cell were able to hold a windmill, the monks of the Chora could grind a lot of flour." Some minor repairs may have occurred in the late thirteenth or early fourteenth century. A daughter of Emperor Michael VIII, Maria, who assumed the name Melanie when she became a nun, and is represented in the Deesis mosaic in the narthex, is known to have contributed to the monastery. She may have also sponsored some repairs.

The next phase in the building's history, however, is the most important and best documented. Around 1315 or 1316 the statesman and scholar Theodore Metochites undertook the restoration and renovation of the Chora. He had been appointed *ktetor* (founder) of the monastery by the reigning emperor, Andronikos II Palaiologos. Proud to be the first non-imperial founder of an imperial monastery, Metochites' presence is visible throughout the building. His portrait survives above the entrance to the naos, where he is shown offering the church to Christ, and his monograms appear inside and outside. His work was completed by 1321.

Metochites, probably the greatest scholar of his day, was also Minister of

The interior of the naos, looking east into the bema. The walls are lavishly decorated with marble revetments. Framed icons of Christ (1) and the Virgin (2) appear to either side. The mihrab was added when the building was converted to a mosque to redirect worship toward Mecca.

the Treasury when he began the project; he was subsequently promoted to Prime Minister. After the emperor, he was the richest and most powerful man in the Byzantine Empire. He was erudite, and extremely rich—the ideal patron. He was undoubtedly personally involved in the reconstruction and decoration of the building.

Metochites' contribution was extensive. He rebuilt the naos dome, the cornice of which is decorated with his monograms, and he provided for the entire space to be redecorated, including the surviving marble revetments and floors, as well as the partially surviving mosaics. He also enveloped the older building with new additions. The *pastophoria* (the small chapels adjoining the sanctuary) were rebuilt and decorated with frescoes; a two-storied annex was added to the north side of the naos; two narthexes were added to the west, lavishly decorated with marbles and mosaics; and a funeral chapel or parekklesion was added to the south, decorated with frescoes. At the southwest corner, where the minaret now rises, a belfry was constructed, bearing Metochites' monograms. In his writings, Metochites says that he also provided silver vessels and silk hangings for the church and books for the library.

Although the main church was apparently dedicated to Christ, the monastery proper was dedicated to the Virgin Theotokos (God-Bearer). In his poetry,

The excavations in the sanctuary, mid-1950s, looking east, showing the foundations for the altar and canopy with the marble enclosure for a reliquary.

Metochites refers to both Virgin and monastery as his refuge. Ironically, the monastery became just that. Metochites ended his days at the Chora and was buried here. Ousted from power in the palace coup of 1328, he was banished to Didymoteicho (Dimitoka) in Thrace, where he spent two miserable years complaining about the local food that gave him indigestion, the wine that went sour, and the meanness of the inhabitants. After many pitiful, if eloquent, letters he was allowed to return to the capital, but to be confined at the Chora monastery. He died there in 1332, a broken man, having first taken monastic vows and assumed the monastic name Theoleptos.

The monastery remained important during the later Byzantine Empire. Several distinguished aristocrats and minor members of the imperial family were buried in the Chora. During the Ottoman conquest of the city in 1453, the monastery was one of the first Christian sanctuaries to fall to the conquerors. During the final siege, the sacred palladium of the city, the miraculous protective icon of the Virgin, said to have been painted by St. Luke, was stored at the Chora, from where it was paraded along the Land Wall to provide spiritual defense against the enemy. However, on 29 May, having entered the city by the Adrianople Gate, Ottoman soldiers arrived at Chora, and are said to have cut the venerable icon to pieces. Their interest was not in diffusing its protective powers but in dividing its valuable silver covering.

The church was converted to a mosque between 1495 and 1511 by Hadım Ali Paşa. A mihrab was added in the main apse, and the belfry was replaced by a minaret. The new name "Kariye" is the Arabic translation of the name Chora, meaning village or countryside.

A German visitor, Stephan Gerlach, described the Kariye in 1568, when the monastic gate and a cistern still survived south of the building, where

The stained glass fragments from the apse excavations. Exceptional in Byzantium, stained glass technology may have been imported from Western Europe in the twelfth century.

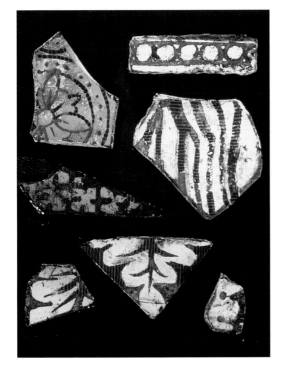

Mosquée Kahrié. 1979.

Salut de Constantinople.

An early postcard shows the appearance of the Kariye Camii before the earthquake of 1894, in which part of the minaret collapsed.

The archaeological plan shows the earliest foundations of Phases I–II (sixth–ninth centuries), the eastern foundations of the Phase III apse (eleventh century), the walls of the Phase III naos, the corner piers of the Phase IV naos (twelfth century); the many additions of the Phase V church (fourteenth century); and later Byzantine modifications, identified as Phase VI (mostly fourteenth century).

the Kariye Hotel now stands. More importantly, Gerlach informs us that the mosaics and frescoes remained visible. Apparently, they were covered with plaster and paint only in the seventeenth or eighteenth centuries—as with the mosaics of Hagia Sophia—and then never entirely concealed. Although we often think of Islam as an aniconic religion, without figural art, it appears that the Kariye's decorations were tolerated through its first cen turies as a mosque.

During the late nineteenth century, as Istanbul became a popular tourist destination, the building became known as the "Mosaic Mosque." The mosaics in the domes were still visible, but those lower on the walls were covered by wooden doors, which the custodian would open for a little *bahşiş* (a tip). In this condition, the building was studied by Feodor Shmit of the Russian Archaeological Institute in Constantinople in the early twen tieth century.

In 1945 the building was secularized to become a museum, under the jurisdiction of the Ayasofya Museum. In 1948 the Byzantine Institute of America, and subsequently the Dumbarton Oaks Field Committee, under took the cleaning and conservation of the mosaics and frescoes and the structure itself, and limited excavations. The work lasted throughout the 1950s, resulting in a magnificent three-volume study by Prof. Paul A. Underwood, published in 1968. A separate volume of studies was published in 1975, edited by Prof. Underwood, followed by a study of the sculptural decoration by the Danish scholar Øystein Hjort, which appeared in the 1979 Dumbarton Oaks Papers. A monograph on the architecture by the present author was published by Dumbarton Oaks in 1987.

Finally, mention must be made of Mr. Çelik Gülersoy and the Turkish Touring and Automobile Club, who were responsible for face-lifting the sur rounding neighborhood, including restoring wooden houses, erecting new, historicizing buildings, and landscaping. These have made the Kariye a pleasant place to visit and an object of pride for local inhabitants.

N ━━━━━

0 ┠─┼─┼─┼─┼─┼─┼─┼─┼─┼─┨ 10 M

phase 1   phase 2   phase 3   phase 4   phase 5   phase 6

Substructure

Superstructure

A domical vault of the inner narthex, showing *The Presentation of the Virgin in the Temple* (**22**). Representative of the innovative style of the Kariye, figures move dramatically and some elements of the narrative are stretched and contorted, with extra figures, trees, and buildings added to fill out the unusual, circular composition.

I. A FIRST LOOK: THE PROGRAM OF THE DECORATION

Examination of the Kariye normally results in a stiff neck from too much looking up, puzzling over the iconography of the mosaics and frescoes. Before studying the scenes in more detail, it is useful to understand their sequence and style. The artists began with the mosaics in the naos, then continued with the mosaic narratives and icons in the narthexes, concluding with the frescoes of the parekklesion. A trained eye can see a stylistic progression as the frescoes become more exuberant and mannered. Theodore Metochites seems to have provided "hothouse conditions" for the painters to develop their personal style, marking a critical point in the history of Byzantine art.

The painting style has been eloquently described by Austrian art historian Otto Demus. He noted that the art seems to have no acknowledged canons, as if the artists preferred the abnormal to the normal, the distorted to the regular, the chaotic to the harmonious. On scrutiny, however, it reveals a canon of taste as well defined as sixteenth-century Italian Mannerism. In compositions, decoration is used to join otherwise disparate elements, adjusting to fit irregular spaces. The architectural backdrops are like stage sets, replete with draperies, shrubbery, and incidental details. The tendency is toward the disintegration of the composition; equilibrium is replaced by asymmetry, instability, and unrest. Figures have contorted postures, and sometimes seem to fly, their draperies fluttering in lively arabesques.

In part, the mannered style was a response to the architecture. Fitting the narrative scenes onto the domical vaults and pendentives (the triangular corners joining the vault to the arches) encouraged the distortion of the composition, as in the inner narthex. At the same time, the artists experimented with compositions and figures. The compositions are based on the accumulation of details, and the whole is held together by a decorative veneer. A domical vault of the inner narthex, showing *The Presentation of the Virgin in the Temple* (**22**) is representative of the innovative style of the Kariye, figures move dramatically and some elements of the narrative are stretched and contorted, with extra figures, trees, and buildings added to fill out the unusual, circular composition.

Theodore Metochites explained the main purpose of the decoration of the church as "to relate, in mosaics and painting, how the Lord Himself became a mortal man on our behalf." Accordingly, the elaborate program includes Old Testament ancestors of Christ, Old Testament prefigurations of the Virgin foretelling the miraculous virgin birth, cycles of the lives of the Virgin and Christ, and the Last Judgment.

The Naos

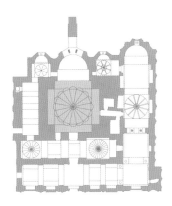

The delicate icon of the Virgin (2) holding the infant was paired with an image of Christ. These icons were both framed and set to either side of the templon screen, which separated the naos from the bema.

The naos preserves most of its fourteenth-century marble revetments but few mosaics. The vaults and upper walls were probably decorated with the major scenes from the lives of Christ and the Virgin, the so-called Dodekaorton or Feast Cycle, as was standard in a Byzantine Church, along with a bust of Christ in the Dome and the Virgin enthroned in the apse. Some decorative mosaics survive in the reveals of the windows.

1–2 Left and right of the sanctuary are framed mosaic icons of Christ (**1**) and the Virgin (**2**), who are shown in pendant images throughout the building. Both are damaged. The figures are identified by inscriptions, which accompany their images throughout the building. Christ's inscription is only partially preserved but originally read as "Dwelling-place (*chora*) of the Living." The Virgin is inscribed "Dwelling-place (*chora*) of the Uncontainable." Both play on the name of the monastery, Chora, giving it a mystical meaning as appellations of the Virgin and Christ. Christ is depicted holding the gospels open at Matthew 11:28: "Come unto me, all ye that labor and are heavy laden, and I will give you rest." The image of the Virgin is a common iconic type known as the Hodegetria, believed to be based on a portrait painted by St. Luke.

3 The only remaining part of this decorative program is the *Koimesis*, or *Dormition of the Virgin*, above the western entrance. This panel had been plastered and painted to resemble marble and was thus preserved. Following a common Byzantine iconography, the Virgin lies on a funeral bier and is surrounded by the Apostles and other mourners. Behind her is Christ, who has descended in a blaze of glory to carry her soul—represented as a swaddled infant—up to heaven. Christ is garbed in gilded drapery, surrounded by a mandorla filled with elegant grisaille angels.

The *Koimesis* or *Dormition of the Virgin* (**3**) appears in a framed panel above the west door of the naos.

The Narthexes: Dedicatory Images and Domes

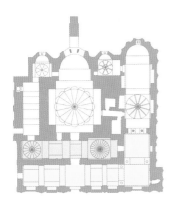

Numerous iconic images also fill the narthexes. Many reflect the dual dedication of the church and monastery to the Virgin and Christ. They also provided points of focus for private devotions within the church. Stylistically, they are simpler and more monumental than the narrative scenes.

4   On entering the building from the west, one is confronted by a monumental image of *Christ Pantokrator* (or Judge of All) above the door to the inner narthex. He holds the gospel in one hand and gestures with the other. The inscription reads "Jesus Christ, Dwelling-Place of the Living."

5   Facing Christ is the pendant image of *The Virgin Blachernitissa*, directly above the main entrance. She is adored by angels and represented with the Christ child in her womb—"bearing what the spacious fields of heaven could not contain," as a Byzantine poet described her. Accordingly, she is inscribed "Mother of God, Dwelling-Place (or Container) of the Uncontainable." This particular type of the Virgin is sometimes called a Blachernitissa, as it was apparently modeled on a venerated icon housed in the nearby church of the Blachernae.

6   Continuing into the inner narthex, one finds above the entrance to the naos the image of the *Enthroned Christ and the Donor*. Theodore Metochites kneels and presents a model of the church to a seated Christ. In Byzantine art, this was the standard way of representing an architectural donation. Metochites is ostentatiously garbed and wears a high hat symbolizing his high office (not only Turks wore turbans), and his court titles are inscribed behind him. The picture is curiously unbalanced, with the side opposite Metochites left empty, with the gold tesserae laid in a scalloped pattern.

7   Immediately to the right is the large and unique *Deesis* mosaic, which shows Christ and the Virgin with two previous benefactors of the monastery kneeling at their feet. Christ is inscribed "O Chalkites"—the Brazen One—indicating that this image was modeled after that on the Bronze Gate to the Great Palace; it is an image with imperial associations. The Virgin gestures to Christ in intercession for the benefactors. At the feet of the Virgin kneels Isaak Komnenos (1093–ca. 1152), identified in the inscription as the son of Alexios and porphyrogennetos—born in the purple chamber of the Great Palace. At the feet of Christ is a nun named in the inscription as Melanie, the Lady of the Mongols. She may be identified as the illegitimate daughter of Michael VIII, originally named Maria, who lived in the late thirteenth and early fourteenth centuries, and was married in a diplomatic maneuver to the Mongol Khan Abaga in 1265. After his death she returned to Constantinople, where she founded the nunnery known as the Mouchliotissa, whose tiny church is still functioning.

Identified as the "Dwelling-Place (Chora) of the Living," *Christ Pantokrator* (**4**) is depicted above the entrance to the inner narthex.

The Virgin Blachernitissa (**5**) is set on the arch of the main entrance, with scenes of *The Multiplication of the Loaves* (**49**) and *The Miracle at Cana* (**48**) appearing in the vault above.

Represented with Christ in her womb, *The Virgin Blachernitissa* (**5**) is inscribed the "Container (Chora) of the Uncontainable."

Sometimes called the *Deesis* (**7**), the mosaic depicts Christ and the Virgin on a colossal scale. At their feet appear two previous benefactors of the monastery, the crown prince Isaak Komnenos, and the nun Melanie.

The *Deesis* mosaic is taller than the space it occupies; visitors find themselves pressed against the back wall of the narthex in order to see it. But it was meant to be viewed at an angle, from the entrance to the inner narthex. Accordingly, there is a kind of reverse perspective in the figures, which are larger on the right than the left, to adjust them to the viewer's oblique view.

8 The terminal bays of the inner narthex are covered by pumpkin domes on tall drums, their fluted surfaces decorated with mosaic. The two function as a pair, with medallions of Christ and the Virgin at the crowns, surrounded by Christ's Old Testament ancestry, organized in two registers. The south dome, above the *Deesis* mosaic, bears a bust of Christ, turned very slightly off the axis of the building. Directly below him, the genealogy begins with Adam, identified by his long beard, with Abel to his right, and the line-up proceeding clockwise with thirty-eight figures.

9 The north dome has a bust of the Virgin, surrounded by the royal ancestry. She is similarly turned slightly off axis, with the regally garbed figure of David directly below her and Solomon to his right, continuing with twenty-six figures.

Above the main entrance to the naos, *The Enthroned Christ and the Donor* (**6**) shows Theodore Metochites presenting the church to Christ.

10 Framed icons of standing saints decorated the pilasters of the outer narthex, although only a few details survive. The Virgin and John the Baptist flank the main entrance. To the north is a partially preserved image of St. Anne, the Virgin's mother; she is paired with her husband Joachim. Preserved behind a column where the sixth and seventh bays meet is St. Euthemius.

The south dome (**8**) of the inner narthex has a bust of Christ in the crown surrounded by his ancestors from the Old Testament in the segments of the pumpkin dome.

11 In the inner narthex, the naos door is flanked by Sts. Peter and Paul, the former identified by the keys he carries—an appropriate image to flank the door. You may compare their portraits here with those in the Dormition of the Virgin, inside the naos.

12 Additional saints are represented as standing figures and bust medallions in the arches of the outer narthex. These seem to follow standard groupings of Byzantine saints, and correspond to the saints recommended by the Painter's Manual of Dionysius of Fourna, a Post-Byzantine artists' guide. To the left of the entrance, Sts. George and Andronikos are most prominent. The figures are elegantly dressed, and the artist has shown them from different angles. We look up the skirts of some, with shadows cast on the inner surfaces of the garments.

The north dome (**9**) of the inner narthex shows the Virgin and
Child surrounded by the royal ancestry of the Old Testament.

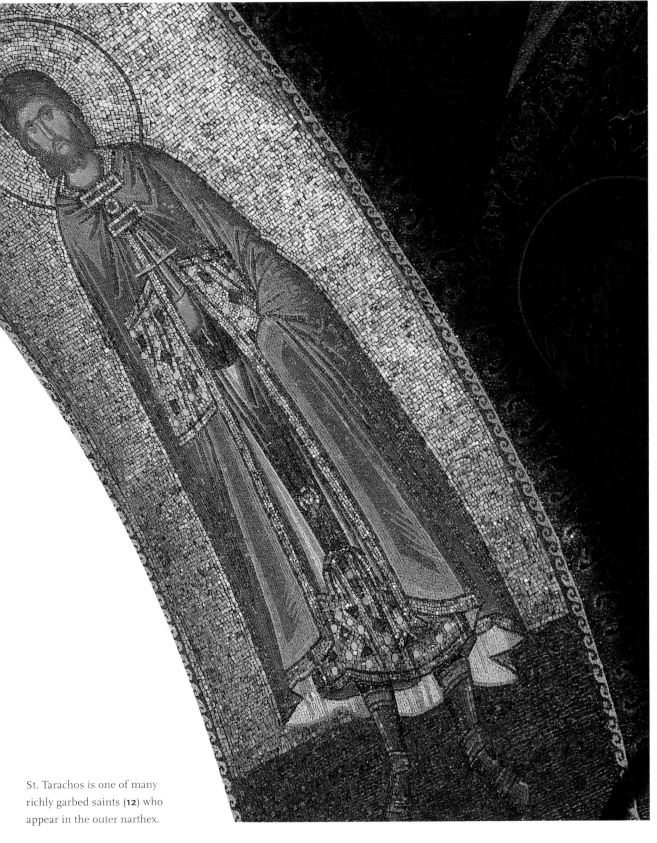

St. Tarachos is one of many richly garbed saints (12) who appear in the outer narthex.

Framed icons of Sts. Peter
and Paul (11) flank the
entrance to the naos.

The Inner Narthex: Cycle of the Life of the Virgin

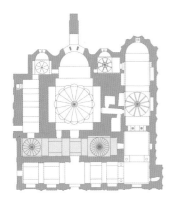

The narthexes are decorated with cycles of the lives of the Virgin and Christ. Both begin at the northern end, with thematic and visual references linking the two cycles. Three bays of the inner narthex are devoted to the story of the Virgin, from miraculous birth to miraculous pregnancy. The unfamiliar subject is based on the *Protevangelium*, or *Apocryphal Gospel of St. James*, which was widely accepted during the Middle Ages. Unfortunately, the beginning of the cycle is broken, damaged by a structural crack in the north bay. Otherwise, the inner narthex is one of the most satisfying spaces in the building, preserving its lavish original coverings on the floor, walls, and vaults.

13 The north lunette, the surface of which is divided by a window, contained an unidentified scene, probably concerning the desire of the aging couple, Joachim and Anne, for a child. A servant peeks out of a doorway.

14 In the northwest pendentive below the dome is part of the scene of *Joachim's Offerings Rejected*. The bearded priest Zaccharias is shown praying in the Temple, which looks much like the sanctuary of a Byzantine church.

15 In the opposite, southeast pendentive, is *Joachim in the Wilderness*. A forlorn Joachim contemplates his misfortune.

16 In the partially preserved lunette below is *The Annunciation to St. Anne*. As she prays in the garden, an angel announces to Anne that she will bear a child. The missing portion to the left may have included a similar annunciation to Joachim.

17 On the arch between the first two bays is *The Meeting at the Golden Gate*. A happy Joachim meets and embraces Anne at the gate of Jerusalem. The scene is inscribed "The Conception of the Theotokos" ("Bearer of God").

18 In the lunette of the second bay, *The Birth of the Virgin* is represented. Anne reclines on a bed, attended by servants who prepare a bath for the infant Virgin Mary. Joachim peers timidly through the doorway. The Nativity of Christ is very similar in composition and is in the same position in the outer narthex.

19 On the arch between the second and third bays is *The First Seven Steps of the Virgin*. The Virgin surprises her mother by walking at six months; Anne subsequently vows that her daughter shall be raised in the Temple.

20 In the vault above, on the western side is *The Virgin Blessed by the Priests*. Joachim carries the child, his hands covered, as if bearing a sacred object. Throughout the cycle, the Virgin is represented as a tiny adult, always dressed in a blue robe.

21 In the same vault on the eastern side is an intimate domestic scene, *The Virgin Caressed by Her Parents*. The architectural backdrops of the two scenes are oddly contorted to fit the curved surface of the vault. Plants and peacocks fill the corners.

Left: A general view in the inner narthex, looking south. The marble floor pavements, wall revetments, and vault mosaics provide a complete impression of a decorated Byzantine interior.

Right: A detail from *Joachim in the Wilderness* (**15**).

Below right: Towards the beginning of the cycle of the Life of the Virgin, at the northwest corner of the inner narthex, is the scene of *Joachim's Offerings Rejected* (**14**).

The Birth of the Virgin (**18**).

The Annunciation to St. Anne (**16**).

22 In the vault of the central bay is *The Presentation of the Virgin in the Temple*. The Virgin Mary is given to be raised in the Temple at the age of three. She is shown again in the same panel, seated inside the Holy of Holies, where she is fed manna by an angel. The western portion of the vault is filled out by maidens bearing torches, the Virgin's escorts.

23 A second scene of *The Virgin Fed by an Angel* occupies the adjacent arch. In both, the Temple resembles a Byzantine church sanctuary, with the Virgin seated on the altar, below a canopy.

Here the cycle of the Life of the Virgin turns and continues on the west wall. The south bay of the inner narthex is treated separately. On its lunettes and pendentives are the concluding scenes of the cycle of the Ministry of Christ, begun in the outer narthex.

24 On the opposite haunch of the same arch is the damaged scene of *The Instruction of the Virgin in the Temple*. Its composition was similar to the previous scene.

25 In the west lunette of the central bay, facing the Metochites panel, is *The Virgin Receiving a Skein of Purple Wool*. The Virgin is presented with wool, symbolizing her purity, with which she is to weave the veil of the Temple.

26 On the arch between bays two and three is *Zaccharias Praying before the Rods of the Suitors*. The high priest is shown praying over the twelve rods presented by the Virgin's suitors. When the Virgin was twelve years old, the priests decided she should leave the Temple. Zaccharias was instructed by an angel to select a husband for her from among the widowers. According to the angel's instructions, each suitor presented a rod, which was left in the Holy of Holies overnight. The rod belonging to the old man Joseph miraculously blossomed.

27 In the west lunette of the second bay is *The Virgin Entrusted to Joseph*. The couple's age difference is emphasized, as the high priest, holding the flowering rod, presents the Virgin to Joseph, with the other suitors watching.

28 In the arch between the second and first bays is *Joseph Taking the Virgin to his House*. Accompanied by one of his sons, Joseph leads the Virgin. Here Joseph is one of the artist's experiments, a composite figure probably created from two different sketchbook models. Is he coming or going?

29 In the southwest pendentive of the first bay is *The Annunciation to the Virgin at the Well*. An angel announces to the Virgin that she will give birth. The drama is emphasized by the position of the Virgin, who seems to be flying.

30 The lunette of the first bay below contains the cycle's two final scenes. The first is *Joseph Taking his Leave of the Virgin* as he goes away on business. The second is *Joseph Reproaching the Virgin*, when he returns from his trip to find his wife with child. These scenes offer interesting parallels to the story of Joachim and Anne, with which the cycle began. Both Anne and the Virgin Mary are blessed with miraculous conceptions.

This leaves the cycle of the Virgin unresolved, but the story continues in the outer narthex with the cycle of the Infancy of Christ.

The domical vault contains two scenes arranged into a circular narrative around a central medallion. On the left half is *The Virgin Caressed by her Parents* (**21**). On the right half is *The Virgin Blessed by the Priests* (**20**).

A detail from the central vault, depicting *The Presentation of the Virgin in the Temple* (**22**). In a scene within the scene, the Virgin is seated within the Temple and fed manna by an angel.

In the lunette opposite the donor image is *The Virgin Receiving a Skein of Purple Wool* (**25**).

The Virgin Entrusted to Joseph (**27**). The scene follows the miraculous flowering of the rod Joseph presented at the Temple.

Depicted on the arch is *Joseph
Taking the Virgin to his House* (**28**).

A detail from *The Annunciation to the Virgin at the Well* (**29**), from the pendentive.

Joseph Taking his Leave of the Virgin (**30**), half of a larger composition that concludes the cycle.

The Outer Narthex: Cycle of the Infancy of Christ

To follow the outer narthex mosaics in chronological order requires one and a half circuits of the space. The cycle of the Infancy of Christ is represented in the lunettes, while the domical vaults are decorated with scenes of the ministry of Christ. Both are based on the Gospels and begin in the north bay.

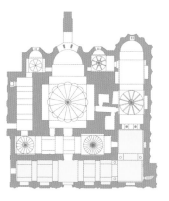

A general view of the outer narthex, looking north. Although not as well preserved as the inner narthex mosaics, two overlapping cycles are represented here, with the Infancy of Christ in the lunettes, and the Ministry of Christ in the domical vaults. Numerous saints appear on the arches.

31 The lunette on the north wall contains three scenes. On the left is *Joseph Dreaming*. While asleep, he is informed by an angel of the truth concerning the Virgin's pregnancy, thus providing a resolution to the final scene in the inner narthex. Behind Joseph is *The Virgin and Two Companions*, engaged in conversation outside Nazareth. To the right, the holy couple begins *The Journey to Bethlehem*, to be enrolled in the Roman census.

32 The cycle continues along the east wall. In the first lunette is *The Enrollment for Taxation*. In this unique scene, the Virgin and Joseph appear before an enthroned tax collector, who wears the regalia of a Byzantine court official.

33 *The Nativity* appears in the second lunette, displaying standard Byzantine features. The setting is a cave. The Virgin reclines on a mattress while Joseph ponders the miracle of the Virgin Birth. The Christ child appears twice, once in the manger, and once being bathed by midwives. Over the hill, angels and the star announce the birth to the shepherds.

34 In the fourth lunette, to the right of the entry axis, begins an extended narrative of the story of the Magi. The lunette contains two scenes: *The Journey of the Magi*, in which they appear riding spirited horses, following the star; and *The Magi before Herod*, in which they are shown carrying gifts and dressed as priests, before an enthroned Herod.

35 The fifth lunette, partially preserved, shows *Herod Inquiring of the Priests and Scribes*. Troubled, Herod searches for the newborn King of the Jews.

36 Turning the corner into the seventh bay of the outer narthex (which joins the parekklesion), the scene in the north lunette is missing but was probably *The Adoration of the Magi*. The narrative concludes in the east lunette with *The Return of the Magi to the East*. This is only partially preserved, showing a rider on a rearing horse.

37 The south lunette of the seventh bay, also partially damaged, shows *The Flight into Egypt*. According to tradition, while fleeing from the wrath of Herod, the Holy Family passed the city of Sotinen in Egypt, whereupon the city's 365 pagan idols were destroyed, leading to the conversion of the population. Statues are shown taking flying leaps from their pedestals. The Byzantines believed that pagan statues were animated by demons, which may explain their vivacity.

38 In the south lunette of the sixth bay, another extended narrative begins, concerning *The Massacre of the Innocents*. In an attempt to remove his potential rival Christ, Herod orders the massacre, and his soldiers set out in pursuit of innocent Jewish children. The small window in the panel is original, opening into the belfry (subsequently minaret) stairs. In his search, one soldier peers into the window.

39 In the west lunette of the sixth bay, the massacre continues with *The Soldiers Slaying the Children*. The narrative focuses on details to represent the massacre.

40 The narrative continues in the west lunette of the fifth bay, which shows *The Mothers Mourning Their Children*. Again, the evocative vignettes convey the emotion of the scene. Grief is shown in the women's gestures and expressions as they hold their slain and dismembered offspring.

The Enrollment for Taxation (**32**).
The Nativity (**33**).

41 The narrative concludes in the fourth lunette, showing *The Flight of Elizabeth and John*. With a soldier in hot pursuit, his sword raised, Elizabeth and her son, the future John the Baptist, escape miraculously when a mountain opens up to hide them.

42 The second lunette, north of the entrance, contains two related scenes. In the first, *Joseph Dreaming*, an angel informs him in a dream that it is safe to return to Palestine. In the subsequent scene, *The Return of the Holy Family from Egypt*, Joseph carries the infant Christ piggyback as they return to Nazareth. The city fills the right side of the lunette.

43 The cycle of the Infancy of Christ concludes in the first lunette, which shows *Christ Taken to Jerusalem for Passover*. The walled city of Jerusalem fills one side of the space; in the center, Joseph leads the family. Christ appears as an adolescent in a gold robe.

As with the life of the Virgin, this cycle appears unresolved, ending with a transition that leads directly to the cycle of Christ's Ministry.

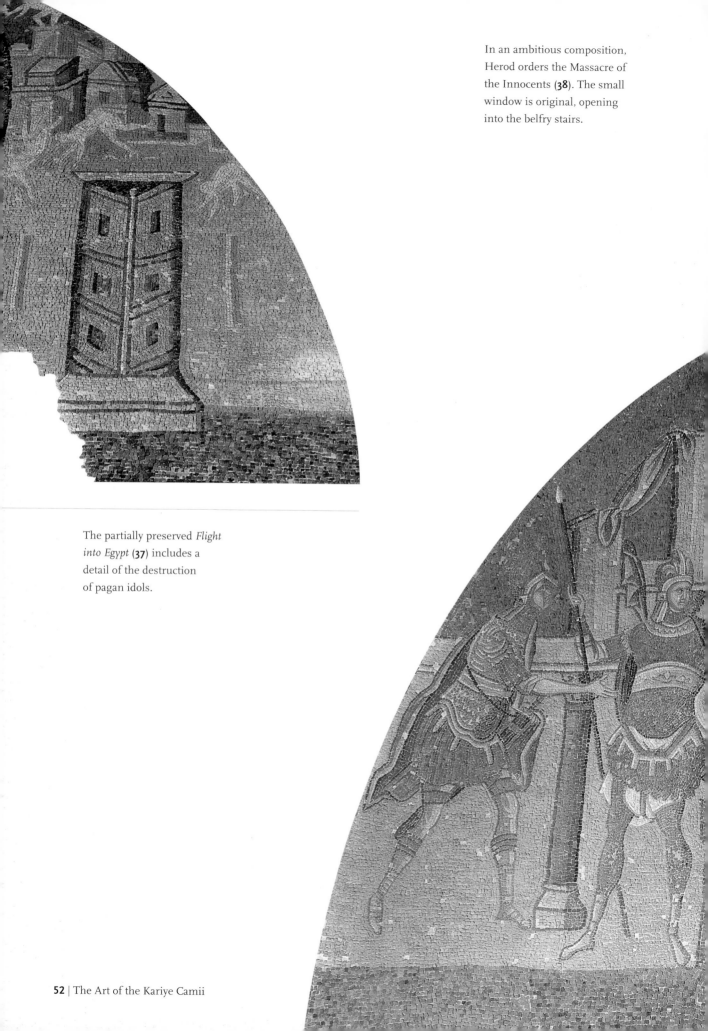

In an ambitious composition, Herod orders the Massacre of the Innocents (**38**). The small window is original, opening into the belfry stairs.

The partially preserved *Flight into Egypt* (**37**) includes a detail of the destruction of pagan idols.

Left: A dramatic scene, *The Flight of Elizabeth and John* (**41**) concludes the cycle of the Massacre of the Innocents.

Above: A detail from *The Mothers Mourning Their Children* (**40**), following their murder by Herod's soldiers.

The narrative continues with two related scenes: *Joseph Dreaming* and *The Return of the Holy Family from Egypt* (**42**). Busts of saints appear in the arch above.

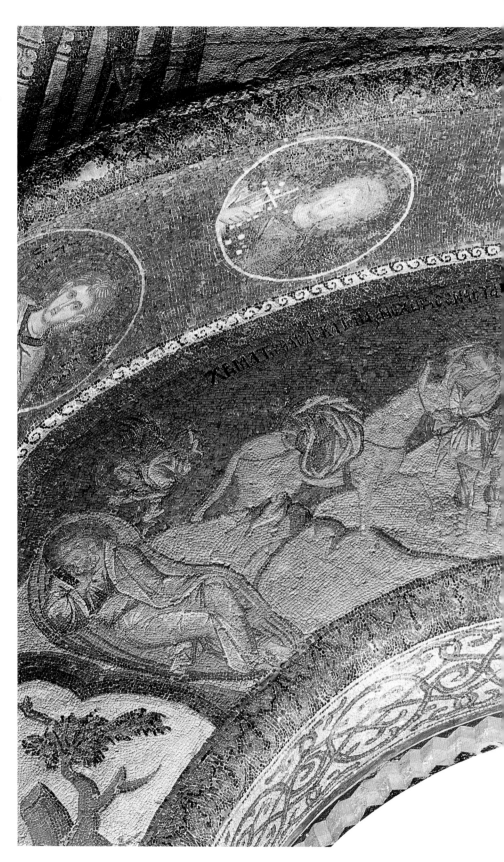

The Outer Narthex: Cycle of Christ's Ministry

The cycle begins in the domical vault of the first bay and concludes in the south bay of the inner narthex. The story is taken up directly from the previous narrative. As in the inner narthex, the narratives are sometimes contorted to fit the domical vaults. Normally two different episodes appear in each vault. Several areas of mosaic are missing, but almost all scenes can be identified.

44 *Christ Among the Doctors.* The mosaics in the domical vault of the first bay are largely destroyed. On the north side are the steps of the synthronon, the seat for the priests in the Temple. The lower portion of Christ's gold robe is preserved to one side.

45 *John the Baptist Bearing Witness of Christ.* The story of John the Baptist begins in the south half of the vault in the first bay. The emaciated legs and camelhair garment of the Baptist can be discerned on the riverbank in the southwest corner. In a vignette, children wrestle on the riverbank.

46 *John the Baptist Bearing Witness of Christ.* Although the well-preserved composition of the second domical vault is circular, it consists of two different scenes. On the north side, John the Baptist gestures toward Christ and testifies to his divinity, saying "This was He of whom I spake, He that cometh after me is preferred before me: for He was before me." In a detail, a heron attacks a snake—perhaps symbolizing the overcoming of sin through baptism.

47 *The Temptation of Christ.* The southern half of the second vault shows four episodes of Christ being confronted by the Devil. In the first, over a box of stones, the Devil challenges Christ to prove his divinity by changing the stones into bread. In the second, Christ is offered the kingdoms of the world if he will worship the Devil; the kingdoms are represented in a small fortified enclosure. In the third, the Devil takes Christ to the mountaintop to show him the kingdoms. In the fourth, Christ stands on the pinnacle of the Temple, where the Devil asks him to prove his divinity by casting himself down unharmed.

48 *The Miracle at Cana.* Although the central portion of the mosaic in the third vault is missing, significant portions are preserved. On the north side are episodes from the wedding at Cana, although the main scene of banqueting has been lost. Table legs are visible in the northwest corner, above a detail of a white bullock being slayed for the feast. In the northeast corner is the miracle of the transformation of water into wine. Workers fill large pithoi with water. The mosaic jugs are made of terracotta tesserae—pieces of ceramic vessels. Christ, accompanied by the Virgin, Peter, and John, gestures toward the pithoi as the host offers him a tumbler, apparently unaware of the miracle that has just occurred.

49 *The Multiplication of the Loaves.* On the south half of the same vault are episodes of the miraculous feeding of the five thousand. In the eastern corner, Christ blesses the five loaves and, breaking them, gives them to two disciples to distribute to the multitude. After the meal, the remaining fragments fill twelve baskets, which appear in the southwest corner. Set on the main axis of the building, *The Miracle at Cana* and *The Multiplication of the Loaves* are given special prominence. The wine and bread refer to the sacrament of the Eucharist.

In the domical vaults is the cycle of Christ's Ministry. This circular composition includes *John the Baptist Bearing Witness to Christ* (**46**) at the bottom; and *The Temptation of Christ* (**47**) at the top.

50 *Christ Healing a Leper.* The mosaics of the next two vaults are almost entirely lost. In the fourth bay, however, one can discern the lower portions of Christ confronting a spotty-legged leper.

51 *Christ Healing the Paralytic at the Pool of Bethesda.* The large domical vault at the southwest corner of the building originally contained eight scenes of Christ's healing miracles, of which significant portions of three remain. In two related episodes in the northeast corner, the paralytic sits stiffly in bed; miraculously cured, he carries the bed frame on his back.

52 In the southwest corner of the same vault is *Christ Healing the Paralytic at Capernaum*. Christ addresses the paralytic, who is richly outfitted in bed and accompanied by four bearers.

53 In the northwestern pendentive of the same vault is *Christ and the Samaritan Woman at the Well*. Other scenes in this vault are preserved only in fragments.

54 Similarly, only small fragments remain of the mosaics in the large domical vault in the seventh bay, at the entrance to the parekklesion. At the south side the scene may be identified as *Christ Calling Zacchaeus*, from the fragmentary tree with figure and inscription. As Christ passed through Jericho, the publican Zacchaeus climbed a tree in order to see him.

From the final bay of the exonarthex, the visitor passes through the north door into the south domed bay of the inner narthex, where the cycle of the ministry concludes with eight miracle scenes.

55 In the southwest pendentive is *Christ Healing a Blind and Dumb Man*. Christ, standing with St. Peter, gestures toward the afflicted man, who points toward his eyes.

56 In the parallel scene in the northwest pendentive, is *Christ Healing Two Blind Men*. Accompanied by two apostles, Christ gestures toward two seated sightless men.

57 In the opposite pendentives, the healing miracles involve women. The northeast pendentive contains the scene of *Christ Healing Peter's Mother-in-Law*. She is seated in bed, while Peter stands to her side, and Christ grasps her by the wrist.

58 *Christ Healing the Woman with the Issue of Blood* appears in the southeast pendentive. In the unusual composition, the afflicted woman lies prostrate on the ground, touching the hem of Christ's garment, as he turns to address her.

59 On the eastern side of the southernmost arch is *Christ Healing the Man with the Withered Hand*. The man holds his deformed arm toward Christ, who gestures toward him.

60 On the western side of the same arch is *Christ Healing a Leper*. The latter wears a loincloth and is recognizable by his spots. The figure of Christ is missing except for his feet.

61 Another scene of healing appeared on the southern lunette. Christ was represented to one side of the small window and is partially preserved, as is part of the inscription. The opposite side, showing the unknown afflicted, has been lost.

The central vault pairs *The Miracle at Cana* (**48**), shown in detail, with *The Multiplication of the Loaves*.

A detail from *Christ Healing the Paralytic at Capernaum* (**51**), from the southeast domical vault. The hollow tube at the center of the composition functioned as a "weep hole" to prevent the build-up of moisture in the masonry behind the vault. These tubes are evident throughout the building.

Although part of the composition is lost, this detail shows the elegant medallion from the crown of the vault and *Christ Healing the Paralytic at Capernaum* (**52**).

62 The large, well-preserved lunette on the west wall of the bay shows *Christ Healing a Multitude* in a particularly fine composition. Christ, accompanied by apostles, addresses a group that includes three seated men: a blind cripple with a hand crutch, a blind man, and another with a distended tumor. Behind them, a woman presents her child with deformed legs; another woman and child appear behind her. In the group of standing figures to the right are a crippled man, a blind woman, and a woman leaning on a stick.

The narrative cycle concludes in the inner narthex beneath the dome containing the early ancestors of Christ, which we may also regard as the beginning of the successive cycles. The narrative cycles have, in effect, come full circle, emphasizing the divine plan of salvation. Their culmination would have been scenes of the Passion of Christ in the naos, which are now lost.

Christ Healing a Blind and Dumb Man (**55**). The extensive cycle of Christ's Ministry concluded in the south bay of the inner narthex.

Christ Healing the Woman with the Issue of Blood (**58**).

*Christ Healing the Man with
the Withered Hand* (**59**).

*Christ Healing St. Peter's
Mother-in-Law* (**57**). On the
adjacent arch is a scene of
the Virgin in the Temple (**23**).

Christ Healing a Leper (**60**).

Christ Healing a Multitude (**62**).

The Parekklesion: Prefigurations of the Virgin and Themes of Resurrection and Judgment

Like the narthexes, the program of the parekklesion is divided between the Virgin and Christ. Here, however, the overriding theme is salvation, befitting a funeral chapel. Arched tombs, or arcosolia, line the chapel walls, which are decorated with fresco rather than mosaic and marble revetments. The lower walls are painted to resemble marble paneling, forming a dado zone, and the walls filled with standing figures of saints. The western domed bay is devoted to the Virgin; the upper walls represent Old Testament prefigurations of the Virgin, emphasizing her role in Salvation. The scenes and inscribed verses are drawn from special readings on the Virgin's feast days. The eastern bay is devoted to the Last Judgment. The complex program of the chapel culminates in the conch of the apse, where the *Anastasis* (Harrowing of Hell) is represented, flanked by scenes of resurrection.

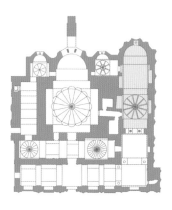

A general view into the parekklesion, looking east. The tomb of Theodore Metochites ("A" on map on page 9) was set under the first arch on the left.

63 *The Virgin and Child and Attendant Angels.* The dome is treated as a heavenly zone, with the Virgin appearing as the Queen of Heaven. She is represented in the medallion at the dome's apex in bust form holding a half-length Christ child, who wears gilt vestments and makes signs of blessing with both hands. Within the dome's segments are twelve angels, who form a sort of guard of honor, wearing brightly-colored costumes of the Byzantine court. The dome's ribs are decorated with rich and varied ornamental motifs.

64 In the pendentives below the dome are four seated figures, shown writing. These are the Four Hymnographers, Byzantine poets noted for their hymns honoring the Virgin. Several also wrote verses included in the funeral service. Of these, *John of Damascus*, in the northeast pendentive, is the most famous, a theologian active in the eighth century. He is identified by his turban and is depicted writing the Idiomela for the funeral service.

65 In the southeast pendentive is *Kosmas the Poet*, a student of John of Damascus, who is shown with an uninscribed book in his lap.

66 The ninth-century hymnographer *Joseph the Poet* appears in the southwest pendentive, holding a scroll on which he writes his Canon for the Akathistos Hymn—an addition to the most important Byzantine hymn honoring the Virgin. The verses connect Joseph to the Old Testament scenes depicted below him.

67 In the northwest pendentive is *Theophanes Graptos*, a ninth-century writer who was a monk at the Chora, where he was buried. He was called Graptos, meaning "the marked one," because he was branded on his forehead during the Iconoclastic persecutions. He is shown writing verses from the funeral service, which refer to the adjacent scene of Jacob's Ladder and to the role of the Virgin in salvation.

68 Immediately below Theophanes, in the lunette at the west end of the north wall, are two scenes from the story of Jacob, in which he has visions of the Lord, *Jacob Wrestling with the Angel* and *Jacob's Ladder*. In the first, he wrestles with the angel, during which he sees God face to face. In the second, he dreams of the ladder leading to heaven, with angels ascending and descending, and the Lord standing upon it. *Jacob's Ladder* was regarded as a prefiguration of the Virgin, and accordingly the ladder is depicted leading to an image of the Virgin and Child. The ladder gracefully follows the curvature of the vault.

A view into the dome, decorated with *The Virgin and Child and Attendant Angels* (**63**). In the pendentives are four hymnographers, *John of Damascus* (**64**), bottom left; *Kosmas the Poet* (**65**), bottom right; *Joseph the Poet* (**66**) top right; *Theophanes Graptos* (**67**), top left.

A detail from *Theophanes Graptos* (**67**), who points with his pen toward *Jacob's Ladder* and Metochites' tomb.

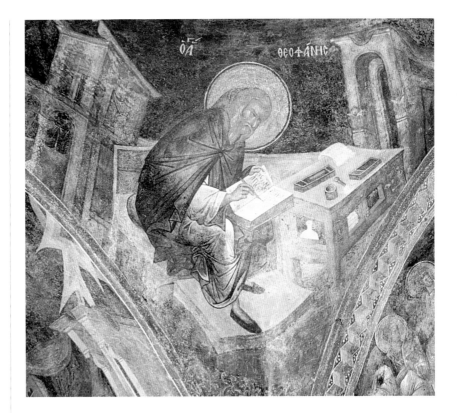

69 On the opposite side of the small window are scenes of the appearance of God to Moses. Within the lunette, the Lord appears to Moses before the Burning Bush; realizing he is standing on holy ground, Moses removes his sandals. On the adjacent arch is a third episode, Moses hiding his face, "for he was afraid to look upon God." The Burning Bush, which burned without being consumed, was regarded as a metaphor for the Virgin, signifying the Virgin Birth.

70 On the south wall of the parekklesion are several scenes from the dedication of Solomon's temple. These begin in the west side of the second lunette, which shows *The Bearing of the Ark of the Covenant*, represented as a triangular-shaped box, to the new temple. Typologically the Ark and the Virgin are related, and the scenes parallel those of the Virgin's presentation and life in the temple, depicted in the inner narthex; both Virgin and Ark are containers of God.

71 On the soffit of the adjacent arch, the procession continues, with priests bearing the sacred vessels, the seven-branched candlestick and the *stamnos* (vase) of manna. Both objects symbolized the Virgin.

72 The third episode, *Solomon and All of Israel,* appears in the east half of the first lunette. Solomon, who is richly dressed as a Byzantine emperor, leads the elders of Israel.

73 The final scene of this sequence, *The Installation of the Ark in the Holy of Holies*, is on the west side of the same lunette. It shows the Ark being placed in the sanctuary of the temple. Light radiates from the sky above to show that the "glory of the Lord" has filled the temple.

Jacob Wrestling with an Angel and *Jacob's Ladder* (**68**). In the pendentive to the left is *Theophanes Graptos* (**67**).

Moses before the Burning Bush and *Moses Removes his Sandals* (**69**).

74 The southern side of the western arch shows the fulfilment of the prophesy of Isaiah concerning the army of Sennacherib, who was unable to enter the walled city of Jerusalem. Isaiah holds a scroll and gestures toward *The Angel Smiting the Assyrians* before Jerusalem. Between the prophet's outstretched hand and the angel, the gate of Jerusalem is topped by an image of the Virgin in the tympanum. Here, the inviolate city is a symbol of the Virgin. Although the prophesy of Isaiah was not read on the Virgin's feast days, the inclusion of this scene may be related to Theodore Metochites' personal devotion to the Archangel Michael.

75 Completing the cycle of Old Testament prefigurations of the Virgin is a somewhat unusual scene of *Three Priests before the Altar*. Originally identified as Aaron and his sons, the fragmentary inscription in fact refers to the burnt offering to be made on the eighth day on the altar, from the vision of Ezekiel. The altar of sacrifice symbolizes the Virgin, and the sacrifice refers to Christ's sacrifice. The priests are shown carrying small boxes and a censer. Both formally and typologically they refer to the Three Magi, whose cycle terminated in the adjacent seventh bay of the outer narthex.

76 Fragmentary remains of a rather unusual scene, *The Souls of the Blessed in the Hand of God*, appear in the crown of the western arch, extending onto the western tympanum. Following the Book of Wisdom (of Solomon), "the souls of the righteous are in the hand of God, and the tortures of death shall not touch them." The composition consisted of a large cupped hand holding swaddled infants representing the righteous souls. Beneath were probably the standing figures of David and Solomon.

77 The eastern bay of the parekklesion, covered by a domical vault, is devoted

to an elaborate scene of *The Last Judgment*, showing Christ's triumph over death and redemption of the righteous—a fitting subject for a funeral chapel. Also fitting is the unique placing of the composition's main elements in a domical vault, drawing on traditional symbolism of the dome as "vault of heaven." A structural crack runs through the dome and has disfigured much of the fresco. Note that Christ's mandorla is now egg-shaped when it should be circular. The focus of the composition is Christ in Judgment. Appearing at the Second Coming, Christ is seated on a rainbow, surrounded by a mandorla of light, as judge of mankind. His right hand is raised, signaling the salvation of those on his right side, while his left hand extends downward, toward the damned souls in Hell. Flanking Christ stand the Virgin and John the Baptist who intercede on behalf of mankind. The twelve apostles are enthroned in symmetrical groups either side, each holding an open book. A row of angels appears behind the apostles, and several rows of angels are clustered behind Christ.

78 *Choirs of the Elect* appear on four clouds that form a semi-circle on the northeast and western parts of the vault. These are identified, counterclockwise from the south, as bishops; holy men, women, and martyrs; apostles, and prophets. Many figures prostrate themselves in prayer.

79 Opposite Christ the Judge is a curious shell-like form carried by a flying angel. This is *The Scroll of Heaven*, described in the Book of Revelation, rolled up at the end of time. Resembling an Ionic volute, the scroll is decorated with the sun, moon, and stars.

80 Directly below Christ the Judge are the *Hetoimasia and the Weighing of Souls*. The first is the prepared throne of "justice and judgment" mentioned in Psalms. Either side, Adam and Eve prostrate themselves in

The Bearing of the Ark of the
Covenant (**70**).

Isaiah's prophesy of *The Angel Smiting the Assyrians* before the gates of Jerusalem.

prayer. Directly below the throne hangs a set of scales, on which the angels weigh the deeds of souls. The souls are represented as naked children, their deeds as scrolls. A trembling figure stands in the center, his fate literally in the balance. To one side a devil (now badly flaked) attempts to pull down one side of the scales, but they are already tipped in the opposite direction—toward paradise and salvation. Other less lucky souls are led toward the fiery stream of hell by little black devils.

81 *The Fiery Stream and the Lake of Fire* descends from the left foot of Christ and runs into the southeast pendentive. Though badly flaked, it is still possible to discern the faces of tormented souls, including several in court dress, wearing high hats like that of Theodore Metochites.

82 In the southwest pendentive is *The Land and Sea Giving up Their Dead*. As angels blow their trumpets, bodies rise from their coffins and the sea.

83 In the northwest pendentive is *An, Angel and a Soul*. Uniquely in this composition, an angel presents a soul for judgment. It has been suggested that this represents St. Michael presenting the soul of Theodore Metochites for judgment.

84 *Lazarus the Beggar in Abraham's Bosom* appears in the northeast pendentive, surrounded by the souls of the blessed. The scene is set in paradise, which has a white rather than blue background, filled with green plants.

85 *The Rich Man in Hell* is set opposite Lazarus, in the southeast pendentive, below the fiery stream. Seated, he turns toward Lazarus to beg for water.

86 *The Torments of the Damned* are represented on the south wall, on the eastern half of the lunette adjacent to the *Rich Man in Hell*. Divided into four compartments, the monochrome figures suffer a variety of tortures:

the Gnashing of the Teeth (badly flaked), the Outer Darkness, the Worm that Sleepeth Not, and the Unquenchable Fire.

87 The north lunette of the east bay is filled with *The Entry of the Elect into Paradise*, the final episode in the Last Judgment composition. The scene is divided into two halves with the gate of paradise in the center, guarded by a red cherub with folded wings. From the left a mixed group of figures, representing different categories of the elect, is led by St. Peter, who applies his keys to the gate. On the right, paradise is white and vegetated. The Good Thief, wearing a loincloth and carrying his cross, welcomes the elect. He gestures toward the Virgin, who is enthroned as Queen of Heaven, flanked by angels.

88 Two thematically related scenes from the New Testament are set within the arch each side of the apse. Both are scenes of resurrection, which complement the *Anastasis* in the apse. On the north side is *The Raising of the Widow's Son*. The funeral cortège has left the city of Nain, depicted in the background, with four men carrying the body on a bier. The widow of Nain's son is wrapped in a winding-sheet and sits up as Christ gestures toward him.

89 *The Raising of the Daughter of Jairus* appears on the south side of the same arch. The scene is set indoors, with the deceased on a bed. Christ grasps the girl by the wrist and raises her to a sitting position—and back to life—watched by apostles and family members.

90 The visual culmination of the parekklesion is the *Anastasis*, or Resurrection, one of the most impressive works of Late Byzantine painting. Set in the conch of the apse, the scene is sometimes called the Harrowing of Hell. It depicts Christ's triumph over death through his descent into hell to redeem the souls of the righteous of the Old Testament who, led by John the Baptist, gather before rocks to each side, as Christ appears in a blaze of glory. He grasps Adam and Eve by their wrists and lifts them from their sarcophagi. Beneath him lies Satan bound and gagged, with the broken gates of hell, its locks and keys scattered about.

91 *The Virgin Eleousa* appears on the lower wall to the right side of the apse. She must have been paired with a fresco of Christ on the opposite side, now lost. The type of representation is known as the Compassionate Virgin. She holds the Christ child on outstretched arms, as though making an offering, and sadly presses her cheek to his. Discoloration from heat and smoke suggest that it was an object of devotion, with votive candles lit beneath it.

92 The *Church Fathers* appear in the apse in liturgical dress, as a church sanctuary. The left-hand figure has been lost, but the others may be identified as Saints Athanasios, John Chrysostom, Basil, Gregory the Theologian, and Cyril of Alexandria.

93 Additional saints are represented full-length and in medallions on the walls. These are primarily martyr saints in military dress, who would have served both as intercessors for the deceased and guardians of their tombs. The two Sts. Theodore appear on the south wall, opposite the probable tomb of the founder. A few monastic and hermit saints are included, with St. Sabas at the west end of the south wall. In the northwest corner is the

The unique composition of *The Last Judgment* (**77**) in the domical vault focuses on Christ in Judgment at the center. *Choirs of the Elect* (**78**) appear in the clouds at the top and lower left. Directly below Christ is *The Weighing of the Souls* (**80**). *The Fiery Stream and the Lake of Fire* (**81**) extends on the right, with *The Rich Man in Hell* (**85**) in the pendentive. Opposite, in the left pendentive, is *Lazarus the Beggar in Abraham's Bosom* (**84**). A bust of St. Michael (**94**) appears on the arch at the bottom.

hermit St. David of Thessaloniki, who spent three years sitting in a tree. An unidentified stylite saint is shown in the reveal of the eastern doorway sitting atop a column.

94 Four additional medallion portraits appear in the crowns of the arches. Within the base of the dome are pendant images of Christ, and a damaged Melchizedek. The pairing emphasizes the position of the righteous king and priest Melchizedek, who offered bread and wine to Abraham, as an Old Testament predecessor and "type" of Christ. A second medallion portrait of Christ appeared in the intermediate arch, also severely damaged. The medallion portrait of the Archangel Michael is given prime position in the eastern arch. Michael was believed to conduct souls to judgment and the righteous to paradise, so he is appropriately pictured close to *The Last Judgment*. Moreover, Theodore Metochites had written a poem to St. Michael, in which he pleaded for the intercession of his soul. The medallion portraits form a distinct group, aligning with the mandorlas in *The Last Judgment* and *Anastasis*, and with *The Scroll of Heaven* along the axis of the chapel vaults.

Above left: The Torments of the Damned (**86**) includes some oddly contorted figures, including one seen from behind, bending over backwards.

Above right: A detail from *Lazarus the Beggar in Abraham's Bosom* (**84**). Scenes of paradise are set against a white background.

Right: The Raising of the Daughter of Jairus (**89**) is paired with *The Raising of the Widow's Son* (**88**).

Preceding pages: The *Anastasis* or Harrowing of Hell appears in the apse of the parekklesion (**90**).

The military saint Prokopios and the hermit saint Sabas are among the many saints (**93**) represented on the walls of the parekklesion.

Sts. Basil, Gregory the
Theologian, and Cyril of
Alexandria are among the
Church Fathers (**92**) depicted
in the apse.

The Parekklesion and Narthexes: Tomb Decoration

The tomb arcosolia represent the Chora's final phase of decoration. Four tombs were provided in the parekklesion, with marble panels slotted into place to form a sarcophagus for the bodies in the lower portion of each arched recess. The upper portions were decorated in mosaic or fresco, and occasionally a sculpted marble headpiece was added. These have cut into the surrounding fresco, indicating that they were added after the chapel was decorated. In some, artists' graffiti were found on the walls. The arcosolia in the parekklesion were apparently filled, or at least claimed, soon after the reconstruction of 1316–21, and other parts of the building were subsequently modified for additional burials. Another tomb arcosolium was constructed against the north wall of the inner narthex, and three of the arcades of the outer narthex were blocked and transformed into arcosolia. The tombs were filled and decorated only gradually, with the last dating near the fall of Constantinople to the Turks. Often overlooked by the visitor, the tombs provide a unique view of Late Byzantine society—and the company that Metochites kept.

Tomb A (see map on page 9), the northwest arcosolium in the parekklesion, was the largest tomb and probably that of Theodore Metochites. It has unfortunately lost its painted decoration. During the Ottoman period its rear wall was removed to form an additional passage between the naos and parekklesion. The elaborately carved marble headpiece was decorated with busts of Christ and the Archangels, which were later defaced.

The most complete of the tombs, Tomb D includes an inscription, a sculpted headpiece, and portraits of its occupants, Michael Tornikes and his wife.

Unique in Constantinople, Tomb G was painted in an Italian renaissance style during the fifteenth century.

Tomb B, the northeast tomb in the parekklesion, has lost all decoration. Roundels of Sts. Sergios and Bakchos appear above the arcosolium.

Tomb C, the southeast tomb, preserves its decoration relatively intact, although the occupants' identities are unknown. Both style and pigments differ from those of the chapel frescoes. Four standing figures appear along the back wall, with the central couple in lavish, courtly costumes. The man wears a tall hat and an elaborate cloak. His wife wears a crown and her dress is emblazoned with monograms of the Palaiologos and Asanes families. A woman in simpler dress appears to the left, a nun to the right. All the faces were restored in Byzantine times. The soffit of the arcosolium bears images of Christ and the Archangels above painted marble decoration.

Tomb D may be identified as that of Grand Constable Michael Tornikes, friend and colleague of Theodore Metochites, who was similarly ousted from power in the coup of 1328. A sculpted epitaph attached to the tomb recounts in flowery but unspecific terms the deeds of Tornikes. This is fitted to a lavishly sculpted marble headpiece. Like that of Tomb A opposite, it is decorated with busts of Christ and two archangels, now defaced. The painting was apparently damaged and restored in Byzantine times, and the arcosolium's surviving decoration combines mosaic and fresco. Fragments of a mosaic Virgin and Child remain in the center, with the finely dressed figures of Tornikes and his wife restored in fresco each side. The soffit of the arch preserves its original mosaics, including a cross at the crown and images of a monk and nun either side. They are identified as "the same person, the monk Makarios," and "the same person, the nun Eugenia." The tomb thus contains double portraits of the deceased, showing them in their positions in society and in the monastic habits of their retirement.

Tomb E was formed by closing the fifth bay of the outer narthex and can be dated ca. 1325–30. Its principal occupant was Irene Raoulaina Palaiologina, mother of the Panhypersebastos John Palaiologos to whom Theodore Metochites' daughter was married. Although their upper portions were destroyed, six figures were originally represented against the back wall, presumably Irene and children. Their lavish vestments are emblazoned with heraldic emblems and the monograms of the Palaiologos, Asanes, and Raoul families.

To either side are portraits of two figures, presumably Irene and her husband Constantine. The arch above is decorated with the Virgin and Child flanked by Sts. John of Damascus and Kosmas the Poet. A burial vault under the floor in front of the arcosolium may have housed the remains of other members of Irene's family.

Tomb F was similarly constructed by closing the arch of the fourth bay in the outer narthex. Only the lower portion of a group portrait survives on the rear wall. Two adults and a child are represented, lavishly dressed. Their robes are decorated in gold, with monograms of the Palaiologos, Asan and Dermokaites families. It dates to ca. 1330.

Tomb G was similarly formed in the second bay, but is different in style and later in date. The lower portion of the painted scene is preserved, with a figure standing before the enthroned Virgin and Child. The figures are three-dimensionally modeled and the throne is set at an angle. The style is that of the fifteenth century Italian Renaissance, and the painting must date to the final years before the fall of Constantinople in 1453. It provides important evidence of the political and cultural exchanges with Italy in the last decades of Byzantium.

Tomb H was constructed against the north wall of the inner narthex. Part of its sculpted decoration survives in the form of two corbels attached to the springing of the arch and decorated with busts of saints. The arcosolium interior preserves a fragmentary mosaic of the Virgin as Zoodochos Pege or the Life-giving Source, with Christ in the soffit above her. Either side are fragments of the crowns of two figures. One may be identified as the Despot Demetrios Palaiologos, youngest son of Andronicus II, who died ca. 1340.

II. A SECOND LOOK: THE ARCHITECTURE

Visitors to the Kariye Camii are usually so impressed by the pleasant surroundings of wooden buildings, lush gardens, and the hustle and bustle of tea shops and postcard vendors that they fail to realize what an odd and irregular building they have come to see. However, the Kariye played a key role in Late Byzantine architecture.

Metochites' early fourteenth-century rebuilding included the reconstruction of the naos dome; the pastophoria; the addition of a two-storied annex to the north, an inner and outer narthex to the west; and the parekklesion to the south. Although these additions were part of a single building campaign, the irregularities of the plan have long confused scholars. It appears as an incongruous juxtaposition of components lacking overall logic. The confusion results from a number of factors: the use of the Middle Byzantine core of the building, the sloping site, as well as the varying functions of the ancillary chambers, caused numerous compromises in the final construction. Furthermore, the six and a half centuries since Metochites' glory have fundamentally altered the building. The most conspicuous change occurred in 1875–76 when, to facilitate the application of lead roofing, tons of rubble were dumped onto the church to level the undulating Byzantine roofline. This "improvement" rendered visually lifeless what was once a dynamic silhouette, and accentuated the irregularities; the odd placement of the inner narthex domes and the irregular spacing of the exonarthex arcade become particularly glaring. Modern scholars have long been aware of this change,

The Kariye Camii seen from the west, ca. 1860, before the roof and domes were remodelled.

thanks to illustrations in the publications of Paspates and Pulgher. Originally the scalloped roofline was edged by a double dogtooth cornice; that is, bricks laid on a diagonal—merely suggested by the drawings, but clearly indicated in a detail of the west façade provided by Pulgher. The similarly scalloped roofline of the parekklesion survives in part; on both, the cornice was partially or totally removed when the roofline was raised.

More precise information is provided by a nineteenth-century photograph, from the collection of Çelik Gülersoy—the only known photograph taken before the renovation. Here we see clearly the undulations of the roofline: the vaults of the two central bays continue over both narthexes, and the two narthex domes sit on separate bases.

Similarly topped by scalloped dogtooth cornices, the minor domes appear in their original forms in nineteenth-century illustrations. When recovered, however, the cornices were leveled, and the domes given a "helmeted" appearance. The main dome was doubtless similar but was replaced earlier— perhaps following the earthquake of 1766.

An exposed barrel vault, still visible in the photograph, covered the north annex, but a sloping roof was added when the rest of the roofline was changed, blocking the small windows in the north naos lunette. Except for the raking cornices, this was restored in the 1950s. Initially the barrel vault would have been hidden by the north narthex dome. Thus, although the two esonarthex domes are asymmetrical, the position of the north dome adds an element of regularity to the north half of the façade.

Metochites' church also had a bell tower in the southwest corner of the building, replaced by the present minaret. Most Byzantine belfries disappeared with the Turkish restrictions on the use of bells and the conversion

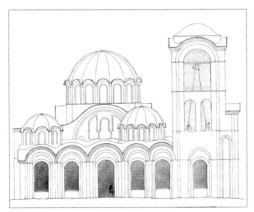

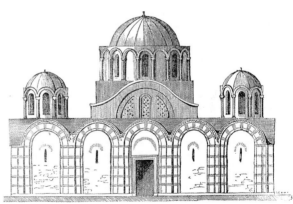

of churches into mosques. We have no written record of a belfry, but it is likely that it covered the entire corner bay of the building, since the original arches of this bay were constructed in double thickness. Evidently ineffective under the weight of the structure, the arches were reinforced, probably a few decades after construction. Columns supporting pointed arches were inserted at critical points.

The extra thickness in the south wall, decorated on the exterior by ogival arches with the monograms of Metochites, contained stairs leading to the upper levels of the belfry. Although such a feature does not exist on any surviving belfry, most were connected to the church gallery, and so did not require a separate staircase. Such was the case at the church of the Bogorodica Ljeviška in Prizren in Yugoslav Macedonia, also from the early fourteenth century, and the Pantanassa church at Mistra, Greece, built in the fifteenth

century, two of the best surviving bell towers. The Kariye's tower was probably similar—at least three stories tall and domed. The stairs probably led
only to the second level, not the full height of the tower, but its exact nature
remains uncertain.

The west façade has also been radically changed. Over time, the arches
were blocked, and within a few decades of Metochites' construction three
were transformed into arcosolia for tombs. The 1950s excavations demon-
strated that the lower portion of each arched opening was filled by a closure
slab topped by a balustrade and was thus similar to numerous Palaeologan
portico façades; for example, the church of the Holy Apostles in Thessaloniki
or the Vefa Kilise Camii in Istanbul.

The central opening is now occupied by the building's main portal. The
sill appears to be a reused and inverted lintel that does not match the width
of the jambs. The jambs are simple, poorly fitted, and face only the exterior—
quite a contrast to the frame of the inner narthex door, made of finely carved
and fitted pieces of Prokonnesian marble and topped by the mosaic of
Christ. Of all the doorframes, only the main portal is so inelegant. We must
conclude that it was added later and that the exonarthex was originally an
open portico, lacking both door and glazing.

Returned to its original form, the west façade begins to make sense. The
present closed, flat-roofed condition exaggerates the irregularity of the plan.
But it is noteworthy that all the spaces are of nearly equal measure, while
the solids have assumed the irregularities. The darker open spaces would
have dominated the composition, visually overpowering the pastel shades of
the piers, and adding regularity to the façade.

The west and south façades of the fourteenth century are shown in reconstruction drawings, which include a belfry modeled after Prizren's Bogorodica
Ljeviška. The belfry certainly alters the visual forms of the building. Rather
than appearing slightly asymmetrical, it becomes clear that symmetry was

A view of the south façade
showing its unusual articula-
tion of stepped pilasters and
half-columns. The rhythm of
the supports is quickened,
with extra half-columns posi-
tioned beneath the windows.

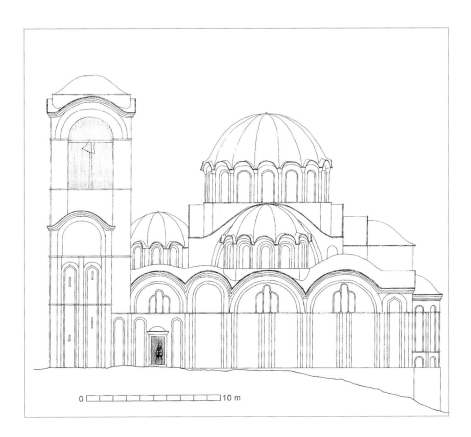

A hypothetical reconstruction of the original appearance of the south façade, with the roof and belfry restored. The drawing underscores the alignment of the naos and parekklesion domes, as well as the alignment of the south doorway with the inner narthex.

not a major concern in the overall design. The building's irregularities vanish amid the wealth of detail, the dynamic silhouette and the exuberance. One was, in effect, not meant to see the forest for the trees. Refinements are localized and small-scale; parts are related to each other but not to the whole; variety is more important than symmetry. The north dome, for example, is adjusted to its position in relation to the north annex, but no attempt has been made to relate it to the south half of the façade; the two domes are different sizes and asymmetrically placed. In fact, no two domes are alike.

The same applies to the walls. There were strong contrasts in the west façade between the dark recesses and the pastel tones of the piers, the latter broken by the alternating bands of brick and stone, and the consistent use of two-stepped responds and engaged columns. All this was topped by the subtle contrasts and undulating rhythm of the dogtooth cornices. The wall was never left as a plain surface.

Our observations lend insight into the aesthetics of Late Byzantine architecture but do not explain the irregularities of the plan. Although appearing almost haphazard, the fourteenth-century additions were built in one construction phase. The approach toward planning fits with the decorative aesthetic, but we must still ask why the building is irregular if it did not need to be. This can be answered by observing the use of the various units which was probably imposed on the building by the *ktetor* Metochites himself, as can be seen in the following.

Little survives of the north annex to indicate its function. The lower level was probably the *diakonikon* (vestry), and provided access from the inner narthex to the prothesis. The unusual upper floor, connected by an internal staircase, may have been the founder's study, housing the monastic library. The Chora's library was one of Constantinople's best and a source of pride for Metochites, who claimed "at the risk of incurring God's wrath and appearing vulgar," that in quality and quantity, it exceeded that of any other

A Second Look: The Architecture | **93**

monastery in Constantinople. Metochites, a writer and scholar, spent much time in the library, and it was certainly given a special place in the monastery. Exactly where manuscripts were kept in Byzantine monasteries is not certain, but because many would have been liturgical texts, it is likely that they were kept inside the church. In the Lavra monastery on Mt. Athos, for example, it is recorded that St. Athanasios' library was above the narthex, overlooking the naos. As we shall see, other planning considerations did not allow a second level above the narthex of the Chora, but the function of this north upper chamber was probably the same. This room is perfectly lit for a library, thanks to a large east window and two to the north. A small window overlooking the naos would have allowed Metochites to observe the services in private. The special function of this chamber helps to explain the lack of symmetry on the east side of the building.

Although an earlier parekklesion may have existed on the site, the four-teenth-century chapel was built entirely *de novo* and was of considerable dimensions, approximately the same length as the naos itself. The most regular feature of the church, the parekklesion represents one of the finest achievements of Palaiologan architecture. Divided into two square bays, flanked by a barrel vault to the west and apse to the east, the two bays are covered by a tall, windowed dome and a lower domical vault. On entering from the west, one is drawn from the dark anteroom to the central space of the first domed bay, where the light is concentrated; this is also the best spot for viewing the chapel as a whole, following the cascade of frescoes from tall dome to domical vault to the conch of the apse. If, as generally believed, the left-hand tomb in the domed bay (Tomb A) belonged to Theodore Metochites, the location was wisely chosen: it was connected through an oratory behind it to the naos and is simultaneously the focal point of the parekklesion. Such careful modulation of space on a small scale is the true beauty of Palaiologan architecture.

Probably the most disconcerting element of the exterior is the placing of the south esonarthex dome, which upsets the balance of the west façade. In general terms, its position was limited to the north by the lunette window and to the south by the belfry. The only explanation given for the large size of this dome is the need for lighting in the south end of the esonarthex; this seems to be an oversimplification. The dome covers a large bay, the largest in the narthex, which disrupts the regularity of the west façade and the sym-metry of the inner narthex; it also dictates the awkward position of the door in the south façade. The bay is deeper than the rest of the esonarthex and is partially offset by projecting piers, which unbalance the decoration of the portal to the naos. Even the marble pattern of the floor sets this unit off from the rest of the narthex, emphasizing its larger size. The iconography of the vault mosaics also differs: the Life of the Virgin stops at the edge of the bay, which is decorated instead with the Miracles of Christ.

However, the emphasis is not on these scenes, but on the monumental and overwhelming *Deesis* mosaic on the eastern wall, a composition that in scale and position is unlike anything else in the church—Christ is 4.20 m. (about thirteen feet) tall. The mosaic's position eliminated the possibility of a third entrance to the naos corresponding to the north door, which

The interior of the parekkle-sion, looking east, showing the cascade of painted vaults. The tombs of Metochites and Tornikes are to the left and right, below the dome.

accounts for another asymmetrical feature of the plan. Although still a part of the esonarthex, this unique space is isolated and treated as a distinct unit.

The iconography of the *Deesis* mosaic is also unique, and could solve the mystery of the misplaced dome. John the Baptist, included in the slightly earlier Hagia Sophia *Deesis*, is absent, probably to focus the attention on the two figures to whom the church was dedicated, Christ and the Virgin. Christ is inscribed "O Chalkites", indicating a typological relationship with the famous image over the Chalke (Bronze) Gate, the main entrance to the Great Palace. This is the imperial portrait of Christ, and the imperial association is borne out by the identities of the two small figures at the feet of Christ and the Virgin. To the left is the twelfth-century prince, Isaak Komnenos, and to the right, Melanie the nun, most probably Maria Palaiologina, half-sister of

Below: A detail from *Joseph Taking the Virgin to His House* (**28**), showing the awkward posture of Joseph.

Below right: A view into the south domed bay of the inner narthex, looking north, with the *Deesis* mosaic (**7**) on the right.

Far right, top: A detail from the *Deesis* mosaic (**7**), showing Isaak Komnenos at the feet of the Virgin.

Far right, bottom: A detail from the *Deesis* mosaic (**7**), with the nun Melanie at the feet of Christ.

the reigning emperor, Andronikos II. Both were members of the imperial family and both were apparently benefactors to the Chora Monastery.

The association of Isaak Komnenos with the Chora is known through documents. We know he had a tomb constructed for himself at the Chora, and it is assumed that he was responsible for the twelfth-century rebuilding of the church, and probably bore the title of ktetor. Later he had the tomb moved to another of his foundations, the Kosmosoteira at Pherrai in Thrace, but specified that a portrait of him "done in my youth in the vanity of boyhood" should be left at the Chora. Though not the same as the Deesis image, it perhaps served as the basis for the surviving fourteenth-century portrait. It is tempting to suggest that Isaac's tomb occupied the present position of the mosaic panel.

Melanie's relationship to the Chora is not documented except for her representation in the mosaic and by a dedicatory poem inscribed in a manuscript she presented to the monastery. We know that after the Latin Occupation, the monastery was functioning again before Metochites' restoration; and it is possible that Melanie served as benefactor and was responsible for restoring the Chora in the late thirteenth century. She also founded the Convent of the Theotokos Panagiotissa (Mouchliotissa) nearby.

This site was apparently set aside in Metochites' rebuilding as a founders' chapel, conservatively adhering to the twelfth-century plan. Unlike Metochites, the previous founders were members of the imperial family; the monastery is referred to as a *basilike mone*—an imperial monastery. Metochites may have honored the memory of the previous founders as a compliment to his friend, the reigning emperor, showing his ancestors and relatives before the imperial portrait of Christ. The emphasis on ancestry is continued in the dome above, where the Old Testament ancestors of Christ are represented, surrounding a bust of Christ. This would also, of course, reflect the pretensions of Theodore Metochites himself, who was something of a social

A general view of the interior of the naos, looking west, showing the luxurious marble revetments of the walls. The mosaic of the *Koimesis* (3) appears above the main entrance.

climber; the figures in the *Deesis* were also his titular ancestors. It is no coincidence that the image of Metochites presenting the church to Christ is above the door to the naos, immediately next to the *Deesis*. Nor is it a coincidence that Isaak and Metochites bear a striking resemblance to each other—within the Chora, at least, they were from the same family.

Like the mosaics and frescoes, the architecture is artfully distorted, chaotic, asymmetrical, and decorative. If we isolate a single figure, for example, Joseph, from *Joseph Taking the Virgin to His House*, compositional attitudes similar to those seen in the architecture are evident. Students of life drawing would cringe at this figure—we are not sure if he is coming or going—yet if each specific feature is analyzed independently, it is more than satisfactory. The artist is composing on a small scale, of individual bits and pieces, and his figure is fine—if viewed in that manner, without trying to relate the pieces to the whole.

Curiously, the art of the Kariye Camii is described in glowing terms like "well-defined canons of taste," "a critical phase, experimental in nature," that "transcends canons of medieval hieratic Byzantine art," and "the product of a great revolution in Byzantine art." The architecture, on the other hand, has been cast aside as tired, mediocre, hardly comparable to the artwork. Is it not possible that such Palaiologan architecture is the product of a well-defined aesthetic similar to the so-called "Mannerist" phase in Byzantine art? And that like the mosaics and frescoes enclosed within, the architecture of the Kariye Camii signaled a new era in Byzantine artistic development?

Dazzled by the wealth of mosaics and frescoes, visitors often overlook the marble revetments and sculptural decoration. These, too, reveal the sophistication of the fourteenth-century artisans. The marble revetments covering the walls and floors of the naos are particularly impressive. Except for some rearrangement in the apse and replacement on the south wall, they are pristine. The Byzantines preferred book-matched panels of patterned marbles, so that the symmetrical patterns of adjacent panels would create evocative patterns that resemble Rorschach tests. Sometimes repeated cuts from the same block create long patterns, as in the dado (lower) zone of the north naos wall. The matched panels of the floor are equally impressive.

The marble most often employed in the revetments is Prokonnesian marble, originally quarried at the island of Prokonnesos (Marmara Adası) in the Sea of Marmara, which is white with distinctive gray veining. A green Breccia, sometimes called verde antico, is also commonly used. The framed panels on the upper naos walls include red (rosso antico), white and black (bianco e nero), honey-colored (onyx), yellow and purple (pavonazetto), red-veined granite (cipollino rosso), and purple granite (porphyry). What is most impressive about this colorful display is that none of this marble came directly from the quarry. In fact, after the seventh century, the Byzantines no longer maintained quarries of luxury stones. Those used to decorate the church are all spolia, reused pieces, and although they originally came from Italy, Greece, even North Africa, for the decoration of the Chora they were taken from the ruined ancient buildings in and around Constantinople. That they have been put together in such an impressive arrangement is to the credit of the marble workers—not to mention the pocketbook of the patron.

Some details are telling. For example, examination of the framed marble panels on the upper walls reveals that many are patched to fit; occasionally similar but not identical stones are set together. This seems to have been common practice, and there is an amusing incident of it in Tomb C in the parekklesion, where the painted imitation of marble revetment includes a painted patch in a different kind of marble. The longer repeat patterns in the dado zone also betray evidence of reuse, for they are rarely composed of blocks of the same width. Instead, the panels are thinnest at the ends of the pattern and widest at the center. This is because they were not cut from regular blocks, but from columns, which were sliced lengthwise.

Another detail indicates that the naos was not originally decorated with marble revetments. The eleventh- and twelfth-century walls actually lean outward as they rise. The fourteenth-century marble workers attempted to correct the angle when they installed the revetments. As was normal practice, the panels were secured in place with metal pins or cramps, leaving space between them and the wall. By increasing the distance between the revetments and the wall, they attempted to create a vertical surface. This failed because at the top the revetments had to fit beneath the shallow, existing cornice, and several bands, including a decorative band of marble incrustation (*opus sectile*), were awkwardly set at an angle to join to the cornice.

The organization of the marble panels in the naos emphasizes the architectural ordering of the space. Above the dado zone, the framed panels form a grid that corresponds with the interior compartments. The opposite effect is achieved in the inner narthex, where the revetments are also well preserved. There the divisions studiously avoid the structural divisions and introduce a second rhythm. The repeat patterns never terminate at the pilasters, and thus create a sort of counterpoint, subverting the architectural order.

The variety of sculptural pieces also includes spolia. The lintel above the main entrance to the naos, below the Dormition mosaic, is decorated with birds and baskets of fruit. It was carved in the sixth century and carefully recut to fit its present location. Two false marble doors lining the passageway at the north entrance to the naos were also carved in the sixth century, originally decorated with framed panels of scenes from the Life of Christ, which were later removed. Other figural sculptures met similar fates. Flanking the sanctuary's entrance, the mosaic panels of Christ and the Virgin were both provided with frames and canopies, apparently original carving of the fourteenth century. The canopy above the Virgin is still quite elegant, deeply carved and undercut, with acanthus leaves curling outward. Although the faces of the figures have been destroyed, we can still identify them as Christ and angels. Busts of saints were represented on the corbels and capitals that supported colonnettes to frame the icon. The corbels survive beneath the icon of Christ, although the canopy has disappeared.

In the southwest corner of the outer narthex, additional bracing was required beneath the belfry. Columns were inserted in a Late Byzantine repair, using four capitals apparently from the eleventh century, decorated with busts of angels and medallions. Despite damage to the faces, they are still elegant.

A detail of a marble capital from Tomb H in the inner narthex, representing a youthful military saint.

One of four eleventh-century marble capitals reused in the southwest corner bay of the exonarthex, decorated with a bust of an angel and an acanthus roundel enclosing a foliate cross.

The marble arches decorating the tombs in the parekklesion are excellent examples of Late Byzantine carving. Tomb H, inserted at the north end of the inner narthex, was originally framed with columns and corbelled capitals. The latter are still in place, decorated with busts of saints, subsequently damaged. During the 1950s excavations, the head of one of the military saints was discovered and reattached. Youthful, with chubby cheeks and jug-ears, dressed in armor and holding a shield, this is the sole surviving head of all the church's sculptures.

Whether new or reused, the marble decoration of the Kariye is thoughtfully integrated into the building. The elaborate doorframes, for example, are probably reused pieces, however elegant they appear in their present locations. Other details are equally elegant. Below the Metochites panel in the inner narthex, a bead-and-reel frame surrounds an octapartite panel in which the triangular segments of veined Prokonnesian marble form a sort of cloverleaf pattern. Throughout the building one can find small cuttings in the marble, where icons, crosses, lamps, and reliquaries were suspended or inserted.

Finally, it is worth noting that many of the marble cornices and capitals were originally painted and gilded. In the Byzantine interior, any surface that was not decorative was decorated. The result represents one of the finest, most opulent, and best-preserved Byzantine interiors.

III. A THIRD LOOK: SPECIAL THEMES IN THE MOSAICS AND FRESCOES

Light shimmers from the gold mosaic in the south inner narthex dome, decorated with Christ and his Old Testament ancestors (**8**). Christ's healing miracles appear in the pendentives (**55–62**).

A Byzantine church was not considered complete until its interior was decorated with mosaic or fresco, usually with complex icons and narratives. The architecture was animated and given meaning by the painting. The selection and placing of images interacted with the services celebrated in the church to emphasize the message of the liturgy. The Chora displays a close interaction between the architecture and the mosaics and frescoes, suggesting a direct working relationship between artist and mason. Perhaps a single master guided both. Certainly, the active presence of the learned patron, Theodore Metochites, would also have encouraged a unity of expression.

One result is the selection of vaulting forms to best display the mosaic and fresco. For example, for the narrative scenes in the narthexes, sail vaults are employed rather than the more common groin vaults, which would have subdivided each unit into triangular wedges, less suitable for narrative. At the same time, the domical form of the vaults caused the artist to contort the mosaics to fit the bowed surfaces.

In major domes, the inner surface is treated in a manner best suited to the medium. Domes covered with mosaic, like those of the inner narthex, are pumpkin domes with undulating, faceted surfaces. The result is multiple curves that capture the light from many angles, creating a shimmering surface and suffusing the interior with a golden glow. In contrast, the frescoed domes of the parekklesion and diakonikon are subdivided with ribs, the flatter surfaces more suitable for fresco.

The interaction of art and architecture has other manifestations at the Chora. Often irregularities in the architecture correspond with irregularities in the art, best appreciated in the south bay of the inner narthex, housing the monumental *Deesis* mosaic. There we can see how the position of images within the building can enhance their meaning. Often the visual juxtaposition of images, set beside or opposite each other, adds another dimension to the decoration.

Comparison is also encouraged through similarities in the position and composition of scenes. Thus, *The Nativity of Christ* in the outer narthex parallels *The Birth of the Virgin* in the inner narthex, emphasizing a common message. Similarly, *The Annunciation to St. Anne* is set opposite *The Annunciation to the Virgin*, although here the responses of Joachim and Joseph to the miraculous pregnancies contrast starkly. In another example, above the main entrance, angels kneel before the Virgin of the Chora. Adam and Eve, who flank Christ in the *Anastasis* composition of the parekklesion, mimic their postures. This provides a visual link between the entrance and the culmination of the decorative program, artfully connecting the parallel themes of incarnation and salvation. Subtle references across the architectural spaces, from one composition to another and from one cycle to another, add to the coherence and intellectual rigor of a uniquely sophisticated decoration. The architecture should be regarded as an interactive frame in which several interrelated themes resonate, rather than an iconographic "cage" to capture a specific meaning.

Generally, the subject of the mosaics is the life of Christ and the Virgin, to whom the dedications are divided. At the same time, the Kariye's frescoes are dominated by two themes, salvation and incarnation, which are directly connected to the dedication of the church and monastery to Christ and the Virgin.

The monastery was dedicated to the Virgin, as Theodore Metochites indicated in a long poem he wrote to the Virgin: "To thee I have dedicated this noble monastery, which is called by thy precious name of Chora." However, the naos was dedicated to Christ, as is suggested by the mosaic of Metochites presenting the church to Christ. Originally, the dome of the naos must have contained a bust of Christ, surrounded by the four evangelists in the pendentives, as was standard in a Byzantine church. This contrasts with the parekklesion, which was probably dedicated to the Virgin, and which offers a visual parallel. The Virgin is represented in the parekklesion dome, surrounded by four hymnographers in the pendentives. The latter are depicted seated and writing, as the evangelists normally were.

To emphasize the dual dedication of church and monastery, as well as the significance of the Virgin to Salvation, there is a sort of "women's equality" in the decoration: Christ and the Virgin appear regularly in pendant images. Their lives are set parallel in the two narthexes, and their images in the dome medallions are matched sets. The *Deesis* mosaic shows Christ and the Virgin with an imperial male and an imperial female donor kneeling at their feet. In Christ's miracles, those involving men are often set opposite those involving women—this is clear in the south bay of the inner narthex. In the parekklesion, scenes of Christ raising from the dead the daughter of Jairus and the widow's son flank the apse. Pendant images of Christ and the Virgin appeared on the walls below. And the parekklesion apse itself shows the *Anastasis* with Christ simultaneously raising up Adam and Eve—the scene was more commonly Christ raising Adam while Eve stands by. Because Christ was regarded as the new Adam, and the Virgin the new Eve, the *Anastasis* provides a vivid culmination to the decorative program, as well as to the sub-theme of gender symmetry.

The dedications to Christ and the Virgin were each developed in a special way, as is suggested in the first set of dedicatory images at the main entrance. Both Christ and the Virgin are given titles related to the dedication of the monastery. Although the name Chora probably originally related to the monastery's rural setting, "in the fields," or "in the country," the titles were reinterpreted to give the name a mystical meaning: Christ is *he chora ton zonton*: "the Land (or dwelling-place) of the Living"—a line borrowed from Psalm 116 and the funeral liturgy—referring to the eternal reward of the faithful in heaven. Accordingly, the theme of salvation is developed in temporal terms, as will be discussed shortly.

The Virgin, shown bearing the Christ child in her womb and adored by angels, set above the entrance, is similarly labeled *he chora tou achoretou:* "the Container (or Dwelling-Place) of the Uncontainable." The Virgin is the miraculous vehicle through which Christ comes to earth and takes human form; she is able to carry the divinity in her womb. Following this, the theme of incarnation is developed in spatial terms. The special epithet is probably derived from the Akathistos Hymn, the most important Byzantine hymn to the Virgin, written in the seventh century, although the epithet is certainly older.

A detail from *The Virgin Blachernitissa* (**5**). She is depicted containing Christ in her womb.

The Akathistos Hymn, a long, alphabetical list of metaphors for her virginity, includes *chora theou tou achoretou*—"dwelling (container) of the uncontainable God." In Byzantine hymnography, the Virgin is frequently called *chora*, normally meaning field—unplowed, unsown fields symbolizing her virginity—and the Akathistos Hymn is unusual in this respect. Variations on the word *chora* are common in hymns, however, with word-plays similar to the monastic epithets, usually suggesting containment. A hymn sung on 16 January, which includes the line, "She has contained in her womb the one the spacious fields of heaven could not contain," encompasses both meanings.

Joseph the Hymnographer, who is represented in the parekklesion, wrote a canon for Mid-Pentecost in which each verse begins with a play on the word *choresasa*, past tense of the verb "to contain":

Alone you contained the creator himself in your womb, Godbearer...
She has contained in her womb the unbounded God...
In your womb you contained the uncontainable Logos...
You contained in your womb, Virgin Mother, the one of the Trinity,
Christ the Lifegiver...

Such wordplays were the essence of Byzantine hymnography, and all the hymnographers represented in the parekklesion employed the epithet *chora* or a variation of it in their poems to the Virgin. Certainly the Byzantine visitor to the Chora would have immediately understood the symbolism of the Virgin as container or dwelling place.

The mosaic depicts the Virgin with the Christ child in her womb—containing the uncontainable divinity. The image is sometimes called the Blachernitissa, after the icon kept in the nearby imperial Blachernae church. There a miraculous icon was housed alongside the important relic of the robe of the Virgin, and this association might explain why in the Chora image the Virgin's robe is so prominent, cascading over the entrance.

In the Chora mosaics, the theme of incarnation is expressed in spatial terms, with numerous references to the Virgin as "Container of the Uncontainable." This first appears in the scenes of *The Miracle at Cana* and *The Multiplication of the Loaves*. In both, containment is expressed by large vessels—pithoi of wine and baskets of bread—that fill the pendentives. Bread and wine, symbolizing the body and blood of Christ, are inside containers, powerfully juxtaposed against the image of the Virgin as "Container of the Uncontainable."

Bread and wine are also the elements of the Eucharist, representing Christ's sacrifice for the redemption of man's sins. These images begin what we

The Multiplication of the Loaves (**49**). Prominent images of containers of bread and wine are set opposite the image of *The Virgin Blachernitissa*.

might call the liturgical axis of the building, leading from the main entrance to the altar, where the Eucharist was administered as the culmination of worship. We may suspect a reciprocity between entrance and apse, as the Virgin flanked by angels was one of the most common apse compositions, and the lost mosaic of the Chora apse may have been similar.

Along this axis, other scenes support this theme. Episodes associating the Virgin with the Temple appear in the inner narthex, above the entrance to the naos. As a small child, she is presented into the Temple, where she is fed manna by an angel. The Temple is a visual replica of a Byzantine sanctuary, with altar, canopy, and enclosure. The manna refers both to the consecrated bread of the Eucharist and to the Incarnation. In another Byzantine hymn, a kontakion of Romanos the Melode, Christ addresses the Virgin, "I have come down from heaven like the manna, not on Mt. Sinai, but in your womb." She becomes "the temple and the tabernacle of the Lord."

The Presentation of the Virgin in the Temple was regarded as a major church feast in the fourteenth century. It was thus placed close to the other feast scenes in the naos. Although the historical accuracy of the event was questioned, its symbolic value was stressed, representing the purification of the Virgin in preparation for the Incarnation.

Two other types of presentation accompany *The Presentation of the Virgin in the Temple*. Below this scene, Metochites presents his temple, the Chora church, to Christ. Opposite, elders present the Virgin with the skein of purple wool, with which she is to weave the veil of the Temple. Like the manna, the skein of wool is a multivalent symbol, which can refer to the veil of the Temple, or curtain of the sanctuary, or to the Virgin as the Veil of the Logos, another popular metaphor. It might also refer to the miraculous robe of the Virgin, as the scene is visually aligned with the image above the main entrance of the Virgin with her cascading robes.

The theme of Virgin as vessel of the Incarnation is emphasized in other scenes. For example, in the Annunciation, where Gabriel appears to the Virgin at the well, she is holding a golden jug, symbolizing the pure vessel she has become. Above her, in the dome, the prophet Moses holds a golden stamnos of manna, decorated with a picture of the Virgin; the vessel can be interpreted as a reference to the Virgin. In the parekklesion, Old Testament prefigurations of the Virgin include the Burning Bush, the walled city of Jerusalem, the Ark of the Covenant, and other images of containment as "types" of the Virgin.

In addition to the Incarnation, a second meaning may be associated with the image of the Virgin above the entrance. It is also a protective image, related to the Blachernitissa icon. One of the most sacred relics of Constantinople, the Virgin's robe was kept at the Blachernae church. It was credited with protecting the city from the Avars in 626, stopping the Arab siege in 717, and destroying the Russian fleet during the attack on Constantinople in 860. In times of peril, the robe was paraded around the city walls. In the words of ninth-century Patriarch Photios, "The city put [the robe] around itself and bedecked itself with it." Her robe was called the *skepe* (refuge) and *peribole* (covering) of the people. Similar language is found in the Akathistos Hymn, which, according to Byzantine tradition, was first sung to celebrate the lifting of the Avar siege in 626. The Blachernitissa thus offered a potent protective image, and the theme of the Virgin as refuge is one often referred to by Theodore Metochites as he discussed the Chora monastery: "I have made thee, O most pure Lady, my hope and the *chora* for the refuge of my life."

The setting of *The Virgin Blachernitissa* above the main entrance to the Chora emphasizes its multiple meanings: the Virgin is vessel, protector, and portal. She is "the Gate of the Word," the portal by which Christ entered the world, and it was common to associate the Virgin with a door, both visually and symbolically. In the decoration of the audience hall known as the Chrysotriclinium in the Great Palace, the Virgin was represented above the entrance, "like a holy door," facing an image of the enthroned Christ above the emperor's throne. Similarly, the theme was developed in an inscription at the Blachernae church: "The house of the Virgin, like her son, was destined to become a second gate of God. An ark has appeared, holier than that of old, not containing the tables written by God's hand but having received within it God himself."

The theme was also popular in hymnography. For example, John of Damascus called the Virgin "Gate of the Lord, ever virgin." There are also frequent references to the symbolism of the Virgin as a closed door, referring to Ezekiel 44:2: "This gate shall be shut; it shall not be opened, and no one shall pass through it; for the Lord God of Israel shall enter by it, and it shall be shut." Joseph the Hymnographer employed the intriguing epithet *pyle theochoetos* "God-containing gate," uniting two opposing themes in the symbolism of the Virgin. A similar union of open and closed imagery appeared in the Blachernae inscription, in which the Virgin is both portal and ark. The positioning of the Chora icon over the main entrance encourages a dual reading, and the contradictory imagery of container and passage may be a fitting expression of the mystery of the Incarnation.

The position of the image suggests yet another meaning. Although it was common to picture the Virgin above portals, at the Chora she is facing outward, framing the view into the monastery courtyard. She consequently appears as the protector of the monastery dedicated to her. But in Byzantine times, the view out the west door of the Chora also must have included the Land Walls. Thus, this image should be interpreted in a larger, urban context, as a reference to the "Virgin of the Walls," the protector of Constantinople. The idea of the Virgin as the protector of the city is manifest in the Late Byzantine period with the common coin-type showing the Virgin in prayer surrounded by the city wall. In times of danger, icons of the Virgin were hung on the walls and gates of Constantinople as symbols of her spiritual protection. In several scenes at the Chora, a depiction of a city gate is surmounted by an image of the Virgin. In the parekklesion, the scene of Archangel Michael smiting the Assyrians before the gates of Jerusalem has a tiny bust of the Virgin set into the arch above the city gate. Similarly, in the inner narthex scene of Joseph taking the Virgin to his house, the gate of Jerusalem in the background includes a bust of the Virgin in the arch above the door.

The setting emphasizes the rich layers of meaning. The Virgin is simulta-

A view into the central bay of the inner narthex, looking north, showing *The Virgin Fed by an Angel* (**23**), *The Enthroned Christ and the Donor* (**6**), and *The Presentation of the Virgin in the Temple* (**22**).

neously the *chora* of the uncontainable Christ, of the monastery, and of the city—the container and protector of the faithful, and the personal refuge of Theodore Metochites. Looking into the church, we can read the image as the beginning of the rich iconography. Looking out the door, framed by the protective robes of the Virgin, we can begin to understand the special position of the Chora—both topographical and symbolic—within the Byzantine city.

When the city fell to the Ottomans in 1453, the Blachernae church and its sacred contents had already been destroyed by fire in 1434. The faithful of Constantinople still turned to the Virgin for protection, but now relied on a different palladium, the icon of the Virgin Hodegitria that had accompanied Michael VIII in his triumphal entry of 1261, allegedly painted by St. Luke himself. During the final siege of the city, it was carried in procession. The icon was kept at the Chora because of its proximity to the Land Walls and the Blachernae Palace. Ironically, when the Ottomans finally breached the walls by the Adrianople Gate, the Chora was the first Christian sanctuary to fall. Fatih Mehmet's troops are said to have gone straight to the Chora and to have cut the sacred image to pieces. The view out the western door of the Chora, framed by the protective image of *The Virgin Blachernitissa*, witnessed the entrance of the Ottoman conquerors into the city.

Contrasting with spatial themes associated with the Virgin and the Incarnation, a temporal theme is manifest in the frescoes of the parekklesion, the funeral chapel built specifically for the burial of Theodore Metochites, his family and friends. Here we find the promise of salvation dramatically emphasized by imagery that evokes past, present, and future as if occurring simultaneously. Together with the programs of the narthexes, they form a series of interrelated narratives, and the frescoes of the parekklesion serve in many ways as the culmination of the other cycles.

With the dedication of the parekklesion most likely to the Virgin, one might expect the Incarnation to be its primary theme. However, as one moves into the chapel, there is a subtle transformation of emphasis from incarnation to salvation, with numerous references to the subjects represented in the narthex cycles. The Byzantine funeral liturgy also includes images that might suggest the Incarnation, but are reinterpreted in relationship to Salvation. Similarly, the Virgin is addressed in invocations normally applied to Christ and vice versa. For example, Christ is called the "Fountain of Life," an epithet more commonly applied to the Virgin. In turn, the Virgin is implored, "Forsake me not all the days of my life and give me not over to the mediation of mortal men," a prayer more appropriately directed to Christ. Similarly, the Virgin is addressed, "Hail, O August One, who for the salvation of all men didst bring forth God in the flesh; through whom, also, mankind hath found salvation." Rather than focusing on the Incarnation, the funeral liturgy subtly shifts the focus to Salvation. Likewise, the program of the parekklesion begins with imagery devoted to the Virgin, but the message is shifted to the promise of Salvation for the faithful.

The layers of time in the frescoes emphasize the eternal reward of the faithful in the Land of the Living. The past is represented by scenes from Old and New Testament: the prefigurations of the Virgin refer to the

Incarnation, but more importantly emphasize her role in Salvation. There is a similar subtext in the Miracles of Christ, each side of the apse, where he is shown restoring to life a man and a woman, in pendant images. The program culminates in the dramatic scene of the *Anastasis*, which links the two levels of the past, as Christ raises up Adam and Eve. These scenes of the biblical past act as a preparation for the future, represented by the Last Judgment in the eastern domical vault, in which the dead are called to their final reckoning at the end of time.

The interaction of Old Testament prefiguration and New Testament confirmation relates to the larger themes of incarnation and salvation that were developed throughout the church—and in the liturgy too. The Old Testament scenes relate to verses read on the Virgin's feast days, and can be connected to scenes of the Life of the Virgin represented elsewhere. For example, *The Bearing of the Ark of the Covenant*, and *The Installation of the Ark in the Holy of Holies*, prefigure *The Presentation of the Virgin in the Temple*, in the inner narthex. Linking two layers of the biblical past was common in Byzantine art; however, many scenes depicted here had special meaning within the funeral service. The prefigurations of the Virgin were echoed in funeral hymns: she was invoked as ark, tabernacle, and temple.

In the parekklesion's eastern bay, the resonance with the funeral service becomes more direct, with evocations of resurrections past and future. New Testament scenes are concentrated around the apse. The *Anastasis*, based on the apocryphal Gospel of Nicodemus, was the standard Byzantine representation of Christ's Resurrection. Christ strides boldly, clad in radiant white, power lifting Adam and Eve from their sarcophagi. Beneath his feet, Satan lies bound and gagged, and the gates, locks, keys, and hardware of hell are scattered about. Despite the composition's virtuosity, there is an unsettling spatial ambiguity, with the figures behind overlapping objects in front or even appearing to fly—but this adds to the scene's immediacy. The sarcophagi of Adam and Eve, for example, are tipped upward and rendered in three dimensions, so that they appear to project into the chapel, stopped only by the intervening cornice.

Flanking the apse are two miracle scenes, *The Raising of the Widow's Son* and *The Raising of the Daughter of Jairus*, completing the cycle of the Ministry and Miracles of Christ begun in the narthexes. The drama is emphasized by the diagonal lines of the compositions, and their messages heightened by the compositional parallels with the *Anastasis*. The raising from the dead of the New Testament faithful can thus be compared with the resurrection of the Old Testament worthies, and together the scenes act as a preparation for the resurrection of the dead at the end of time, depicted in the vault above.

The unique representation of the Last Judgment fills the domical vault and most of the eastern bay's supporting walls. Here the emphasis is on the future, the "last things"—death, final judgment, immortality in heaven or eternal punishment in the fires of hell. Christ sits in judgment, accompanied by the Virgin, John the Baptist, Apostles, Angels, and Archangels. Christ was originally surrounded by a circular mandorla, but the vault cracked when the foundations settled, leaving the mandorla egg-shaped. Christ raises his right hand to show that those on his right are saved, where-

as the downward gesture of his left hand indicates that those on his left are damned. The vault is filled with clouds bearing choirs of the elect, and with the striking image of the scroll of heaven rolled up at the end of time. Beneath Christ's feet is the Hetoimasia—the prepared throne, flanked by Adam and Eve in postures that reflect the *Anastasis* composition. Beneath, angels with scales weigh the deeds of the souls of the deceased, who are then directed either to the heavenly paradise or to the torments of hell.

In two pendentives, land and sea give up their dead, and an angel conducts a soul to judgment. To Christ's right are scenes of heavenly reward. In the pendentive Lazarus is in the bosom of Abraham, and, on the flanking wall, is the entry of the elect into paradise. The fiery stream issues from the Christ's left side, leading to the lake of fire and torments of the damned in Hell—including, in the pendentive opposite Lazarus, the rich man in hell. Christ's words of judgment emphasize the themes of time and eternity: "Come, ye blessed of my father, inherit the kingdom prepared for you from the foundation of the world." And "Depart from me, ye cursed, into everlasting fire, prepared for the devil and his angels."

A general view of *The Last Judgment* (**77**), with *The Entry of the Elect into Paradise* (**87**) on the left side and *The Torments of the Damned* (**86**) in hell on the right.

The Scroll of Heaven (**79**)
rolled up at the end of time.

Little in the iconography is unusual: *The Last Judgment* follows earlier models. But the scene was normally organized in registers on a flat surface; at the Chora, the placing of the scene in a domical vault is unique and provides a compositional unity and heightened significance lacking in all other versions. The organization of the scene uses the symbolism of the dome: the celestial elements of the composition are set into a "dome of heaven," while those elements not immediately related to the vision of "the son of man in heaven" are represented in the pendentives and lunettes. The celestial symbolism is reflected in the requiem office for the dead, in which Christ is addressed as "Master and Creator of the vault of heaven."

In fact, the dome is so well suited to the celestial aspects of the Last Judgment, it seems remarkable that the Chora's composition was never repeated. The only other example of a Last Judgment set into a dome appears in the narthex of the Panagia Phorbiotissa at Asinou on Cyprus, from the 1330s. There, however, the scene is simplified to the point where the subject is barely recognizable: Christ the judge is reduced to a Pantocrator image, with the other, surrounding figures as busts in roundels.

Both the expressive potential and the temporal structuring of the Chora parekklesion are missing.

The themes of resurrection and judgment would have had an immediate resonance for the Byzantine visitor, who occupied the temporal "place" between past and future. The deceased in the chapel rested in a similar position, in four arcosolia set into the lateral walls. Cuttings in the recesses indicate that the lower portion of each was filled with a sarcophagus of sorts, formed by a stone slab across the front and covered by a lid. As each received the mortal remains, the upper portion of the arcosolium was decorated with full-length portraits of the deceased, enforcing the idea of their presence in the tomb, awaiting final judgment.

The founder Theodore Metochites was probably buried in the northwest tomb, whose decoration has not survived, although its elaborately sculpted frame is preserved. This was the largest arcosolium in the parekklesion and its position was unique. It was connected to the naos by a passageway immediately behind it, and it lay below the tall, windowed dome, where the light in the chapel was concentrated. Visitors who pause to admire the panoramic sweep of the chapel's decoration find themselves unwittingly stopping before the tomb of the founder.

The dome above, decorated with a bust of the Virgin and Child surrounded by angels and archangels, provided celestial illumination for the founder's tomb. Moreover, the tomb had a direct connection with the celestial sphere via the image of Jacob's Ladder, which arches above it. As a metaphor for the Virgin, Jacob's Ladder was regarded as the "bridge" from death to eternity, and is referred to as such in the funeral service. In the pendentive above, the hymnographer Theophanes Graptos (who was interred at the Chora) is depicted in the act of writing the hymn to the Virgin that was part of the sixth ode in the funeral service. Pen poised, pointing toward Jacob's Ladder —and toward the tomb of Metochites—Theophanes writes, "We have turned back to the earth because we have sinned against the commandments of God. But through thee, O Virgin, we have ascended from earth unto heaven, shaking off the corruption of death." The ladder, a prefiguration of the Incarnation, is thus reinterpreted as a Salvation motif. Both the visual imagery and the liturgy, then, weave a complex relationship that extends from the past, Old Testament to New Testament, to the present, and to future Salvation.

Only two tomb compositions survive, both unfortunately damaged and repaired already in Byzantine times. In the southwest tomb opposite Theodore Metochites, nobly garbed figures of the Grand Constable Michael Tornikes and his wife were depicted flanking an image of the Virgin and Child. Represented on soffits each side are a monk and a nun, whose inscriptions read "the same person, the monk Makarios," and "the same person, the nun Eugenia." We thus have "double portraits" in which the deceased are represented twice, once in the elegant civil dress of the fourteenth century, and once in the monastic garb they donned on retiring from this world. The monastic habits, like funeral shrouds, were called "robes of incorruption," put on in preparation for eternity. The dual aspects of their lives are thereby represented, as citizens both of this world and the next.

A view into the parekklesion, looking west toward the colonnaded entrance.

A detail of the north wall of the parekklesion, with *Theophanes Graptos* (**67**) in the pendentive at the top, with *Jacob's Ladder* and *Jacob Wrestling with the Angel* (**68**) in the lunette.

A detail from *An Angel and a Soul* (**83**), thought to represent St. Michael presenting the soul of Theodore Metochites for final judgment.

The "double portrait" may have been carried one step further with the depiction of the founder. Although his tomb portrait has disappeared, in the northwest pendentive of the domical vault an angel presents a soul for judgment, protectively resting a hand on his head. A unique element in the Last Judgment iconography, the scene has been interpreted as the Archangel Michael presenting the soul of Metochites. In an unpublished poem, Metochites implored St. Michael to intercede for him before the seat of judgment. The poem concludes with a quote from I Thessalonians 4:16, "For the Lord himself shall descend from heaven with a shout, with the voice of the archangel, and with the trump of God: and the dead in Christ shall rise first." The same verse was read in the funeral service. If the interpretation is correct, the founder was represented up to three times in different temporal settings.

Sheltered beneath the heavenly canopy of the parekklesion, the dead were included in *The Last Judgment*. As the dead are called forth for judgment, so too are those buried in the chapel. And as the resurrected Christ raises Adam and Eve out of their sarcophagi, the promise of salvation is held out to those resting in the sarcophagi below. In fact, the diagonal lines formed by the tilted sarcophagi lead the viewer's gaze directly to the rows of tombs below and give visual emphasis to this connection. Similarly, Christ in *The Last Judgment* raises his right hand to the saved, simultaneously gesturing

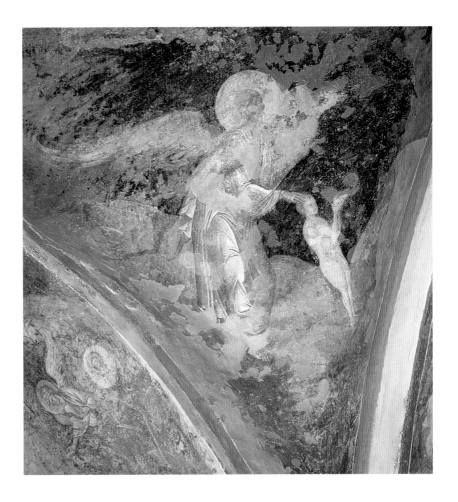

across the vault toward the soul of Theodore Metochites, and to Metochites' corporeal remains in the tomb below.

The same temporal structuring is also found in the liturgy, which blends past and future to promise Salvation to those in the present. In the Anthem from the funeral service by John of Damascus (who is shown composing it in one of the main dome's pendentives), mutable pleasures of the earth are set against the finality of death. Paraphrasing verses from Old and New Testaments, Christ is implored to "grant rest unto him whom thou has removed from temporal things," and to "give rest to thy servant in the land of the living." The land of the living, *he chora tou zonton*, is the inscription that accompanies the dedicatory images of Christ throughout the building. The epithet could be applied both to the monastery, where Theodore Metochites' body rested, and to paradise, where he hoped his soul would reside. Following his troubled life, Metochites could find both verbal and visual reassurance for the salvation of his soul in his tomb at the Chora, where he was surrounded by the prayers of the monks, aided by the intercession of the Virgin and of St. Michael, connected to heavenly realm by Jacob's Ladder, and called to paradise by the Savior. The unity of architecture and painting serves to create a ritual space, in which past, present, and future converge.

A detail from *The Enthroned Christ and the Donor* (**6**), showing Theodore Metochites in his austentatious court costume holding a model of the church.

The donor portrait of Theodore Metochites, wearing his high hat, is one of Byzantium's most famous images. The turban-like headgear, which the Byzantines called a "sunshade," was a symbol of his high rank in society, and his luxurious silk robe is embroidered with gold. His wealth is flaunted, and the inscription announces his status, identifying him as *Ho Ktetor Logothetes tou Genikou Theodoros ho Metochites* (The Founder, Prime Minister Theodore Metochites). His monograms reappear throughout the building, proudly proclaiming his social position and munificence—in brick decoration on the base of the belfry, carved on the bosses of the naos cornice, and painted on the mullion capitals. As Metochites kneels, gazing toward Christ, his expression is bland, hardly suggesting the complexity of the man. Nevertheless, we can find other, more subtle, traces of Metochites in his building and its decoration.

Not merely a politician, Metochites was also a man of great intellectual ability, a prolific and versatile author. According to his student Nikephoros Gregoras, "From morning to evening he was most wholly and eagerly devoted to public affairs as if scholarship was absolutely indifferent to him; but later in the evening, having left the palace, he became absorbed in science to such a degree as if he were a scholar with absolutely no connection to any other affairs." We can imagine him sitting in his library, above the north annex, working into the night by candlelight, listening to the monks of the Chora singing the night vigil in the naos below. Or perhaps more melodramatically, we can imagine him returned from exile to his confinement at the Chora, from where he could see the ruins of his family palace—a sight that reduced him to tears.

Metochites was a prolific scholar. He wrote *Commentaries on Aristotle*, *Miscellaneous Essays*, an *Introduction to Astronomy*, *Orations*, hexameter poems, and hagiographic encomia. His surviving work amounts to almost nineteen hundred folios. However, most of his writings remain unpublished because of his notoriously obscure style, filled with complex sentence structures, borrowings from the Old Testament and Classical literature, a neo-Homeric vocabulary of his own devising, and references to dozens of ancient authors. Many editors have thrown up their hands in despair when faced with the writings of Theodore Metochites.

Metochites was been born into a cultivated household of Constantinople in 1270, not long after the reconquest of the city from the Latins in 1261. His parents started his education early and supervised it themselves. Metochites' youth coincided with a period of ardent antiquarianism, amid a highly literate, if small, society whose members professed an insatiable thirst for knowledge. They loved, collected, exchanged, and copied books; they rediscovered, cherished, and imitated ancient texts; and they wrote their own treatises, developed their own distinctive styles of writing, and corresponded with each other regularly.

The comfortable childhood ended in 1283 with the family banished to Asia Minor, following the death of Emperor Michael VIII, whose unpopular policies Metochites' father supported. They settled in Nicaea (Iznik), where the young Metochites was enrolled in school to learn the Trivium and Quadrivium. The political fate of his parents apparently led Metochites to seek a scholarly life, eschewing politics. Around the age of twenty, he began to write his own compositions.

At this time the precocious young Metochites was presented to the reigning emperor Andronikos II during the latter's inspection tour of Asia Minor in 1290. Metochites apparently recited one of his own compositions, a eulogy to the city of Nicaea, in the emperor's presence. He must have been impressive, for despite his father's disgrace—his father was still officially a state prisoner—Metochites was taken into the imperial retinue.

Overcoming familial disgrace, Metochites' political rise was rapid, and his future inextricably linked to the person of Andronikos II. Within a year he was granted the title of Logothete of the Herds, and membership of the senatorial class. During the 1290s he participated in several embassies, mostly to arrange political marriages for members of the imperial family to neighboring sovereigns. He traveled to Cyprus, Armenian Cilicia, and Serbia. In 1303, when the empress Irene (Yolanda of Montferrat) departed the capital to establish her own semi-independent rule in Thessaloniki, Metochites was sent along as her Prime Minister. Within two years, ca. 1305–6, he returned to Constantinople to be appointed Prime Minister of the whole Empire, as well as Prime Minister of the Treasury.

For the remainder of his political career, Metochites served as a sort of grand vizier, mediating between the emperor and his subjects. In this powerful position, he determined who would receive favors and who would be granted audiences. Having superceded his political rivals, he amassed a fortune appropriate to his status, selling positions, land grants, and titles. He also established closer links with the emperor by marrying several of his children to lesser members of the imperial family.

Metochites did not abandon his literary pursuits, however, and continued to study and write essays at night. He also composed stylized poetic epitaphs on the deaths of the empress Irene (1317) and co-emperor Michael IX (1320). His love of knowledge was apparently supported by the emperor, who encouraged him, aged forty-three, to take up astronomy.

Around 1316 he turned his interests to the Chora, again, apparently at the encouragement of the emperor. His own family palace lay nearby, within sight of the monastery, and both were close to the main imperial residence at the Blachernae Palace. The monastery had been formerly under the protection of the emperor's family but Metochites proudly records that he was personally requested by Andronikos II to undertake its restoration. For all his ability, Metochites was a social climber of the first order. Throughout his career, he did his utmost to align himself with the emperor. Metochites would be delighted to know that uninformed tour guides in Istanbul today tell unknowing tourists that he was the emperor.

The completion of the Chora and its decoration coincided with the height of Metochites' political ascendancy. In 1321 he was named Great Logothete, the highest court dignity, and he rearranged the order of precedence at court to emphasize the importance of his new position over his rivals. He was second only to the emperor in wealth and power.

Unfortunately, Metochites could not enjoy his success for long. He had been in imperial service for over thirty years, and the aging emperor

Andronikos had been reigning for almost forty. While literature and culture flourished within the capital, the Byzantine Empire itself was in serious jeopardy. Most of the setbacks had occurred during the reign of Andronikos II—and the ministry of Metochites. During his inspection tours of Asia Minor, for example, Andronikos—and we may presume Metochites—was more interested in rebuilding the ancient city of Tralles than in establishing an effective defense against the Ottomans. The glories of ancient culture outweighed the urgent necessities of the present. By 1321, the Ottomans had conquered most Byzantine territories in Asia Minor; Catalan mercenaries had devastated other parts of the empire, the Balkan borders were crumbling, and Italian merchants were undermining the Byzantine maritime economy.

With the death of Michael IX in 1320, serious conflicts arose between the emperor and his grandson Andronikos III that developed into civil war. Metochites' fortunes were entwined with the elder Andronikos, but his power over the emperor began to be questioned by other courtiers, by the emperor's immediate family, and even by Metochites' own children. Regarded as the emperor's "evil genius," a plot was formed in 1328 to have Metochites deposed. He feared both a popular rebellion and the loss of his fortune. He dreamed he saw a thief stealing the key to his personal treasury.

So unpopular was Metochites that a delegation of dignitaries from Constantinople offered to deliver the city to the younger Andronikos, on the condition that Metochites would be perpetually disgraced—blinded or perhaps executed. Andronikos III soon succeeded in taking the capital by force, however, obviating such extreme measures. Nevertheless, this ended the political careers of both Metochites and the elder Andronikos. Metochites' possessions were confiscated, his family palace razed, and he was exiled to Didymoteicho in Thrace, where he remained for two miserable years.

Finally, in poor health, a broken man, he was allowed to return to Constantinople in 1330, but to permanent confinement in the Chora monastery. He continued to write, and contemplate his fate. In 1332, having taken monastic vows as the monk Theoleptos on his deathbed, he was buried in the tomb he had prepared in the parekklesion.

His portrait reveals none of the intellectual restlessness, the political triumph, and the ultimate failure of Theodore Metochites. His flatterers called him Philosophy personified. Yet his enemies characterized him as a verbose, incomprehensible bore, who suffered from avarice, a boastful self-love, and an infatuation with his own intelligence. If we look beyond the portrait, however, we may be able "read" in the art of the Chora something of Metochites the statesman, social climber, and intellectual.

Although the expression of the mosaics and frescoes may be intellectually complex, and the style sophisticated, the theological message is conservative. None of the great religious debates of the age finds any echo at the Chora; the selection of saints is also standard. This may express the donor's personality. Metochites' father George was an infamous heretic, who as ambassador to Michael VIII had supported the union of the Orthodox and Latin Churches. A cause célèbre in the late thirteenth century, the union was hotly contested, never accepted by the church, and the emperor was denied a proper Orthodox burial upon his death. Stubborn to the end, George Metochites refused to recant, and consequently suffered excommunication and banishment.

Theodore Metochites never forgot the humiliation of his youth in exile—he often wrote, "salvation lies in safety." Although he relished intellectual debate, this did not include matters of religion. And although he was exceptionally well read in theology, it was of the conservative, Orthodox variety. He frequently admonished himself not to pursue theological problems, fearing accusation of heresy. Thus, despite its boldly experimental style, the theology of the Chora is "safe."

Metochites' concern for his spiritual well being—in addition to glory on this earth—must have been a compelling reason for his reconstruction of the Chora. His spiritual concerns are most clearly seen in the decoration of the parekklesion, which affirms his salvation, as discussed in the previous chapter. The chapel and its decoration offered both verbal and visual reassurance to its founder. In his strategically placed tomb, Metochites benefited from the prayers of the monks and the protection and intercession of the saints and prophets, and he was personally called to his heavenly reward by the Savior himself.

Metochites' political career is also reflected in the decoration. One curious (and unique) scene in the cycle of the Infancy of Christ in the outer narthex shows *The Enrollment for Taxation*. In his position as Minister of the Treasury, Theodore Metochites was responsible for tax collecting—it may have been the wealth he accumulated from tax farming (the system of selling permissions to collect taxes for profit) that enabled him to reconstruct the Chora. The tax collector in the scene is enthroned, wears a high hat, and bears more than a passing resemblance to Metochites. Could this be Metochites inserting himself into the narrative? One scholar has referred to this scene as "taxation with representation." Located to the right of the great mosaic icon of Christ above the main entrance, the scene might be regarded as an example of "good government" at work. It is perhaps the greatest glorification of tax collecting in medieval art.

Another scene in the inner narthex may reflect an event in Metochites' political career. In the narrative of *The Virgin Entrusted to Joseph*, the difference in ages between the childlike Virgin and the elderly Joseph is startling. However, in one of Metochites' important diplomatic missions, he was responsible for arranging such a marriage as this. As a part of political negotiations with Serbia, in 1299 Metochites settled the marriage contract between Simonis, the five-year-old daughter of the Emperor Andronikos II, and King Milutin of Serbia, who was well into middle age at the time. An act of political desperation, it checked the aggressive expansion of Serbia into Byzantine territory, and the negotiations required Metochites to travel five times to Serbia. The marriage raised eyebrows in Constantinople, including those of the Patriarch, but it affirmed important diplomatic ties between Byzantium and Serbia. Thus, in the mosaics of the Kariye, the Virgin is "entrusted" to Joseph, just as the young Simonis was entrusted to Milutin, who through the union became the son-in-law of the Byzantine emperor.

A detail from *The Enrollment for Taxation* (**32**), showing the tax collector dressed as a high court official—and looking a bit like Theodore Metochites.

A detail from *Christ Chalkites* from the *Deesis* mosaic (**7**), an image with imperial associations.

There is also an imperial flavor to the decoration of the Chora, evidence of Metochites the courtier, snob, and social climber. The parading saints are outfitted in the finest garments of the day, costly silks embroidered with gold—the dress of the Byzantine court. Among the richly garbed saints in the outer narthex is Andronikos, whose only relevance was that he bore the name of emperor.

Several images are adopted from imperial prototypes and similarly proclaim the imperial status of Metochites' monastery. The image of the Virgin above the entrance was based on one of the most important in the city, and was credited with its protection. The icon was kept in the nearby Blachernae church, which adjoined the imperial palace, and was a major site of court ceremonial. By selecting this image, Metochites usurped a bit of the imperial aura, placing his monastery under the same spiritual protection. Similarly, the Christ in the *Deesis* mosaic in the inner narthex is inscribed "O Chalkites," indicating that it follows the prototype of the Christ represented on the Chalke Gate of the Great Palace. It is the imperial image of Christ, suitable for the two imperial family members included in the panel, and presumably for Metochites too.

The resemblance of the Kariye *Deesis* with the slightly earlier, imperially commissioned *Deesis* panel in Hagia Sophia is perhaps also significant, particularly in the size of the figures, so out of scale at the Chora. The off-balance composition and the posture of Metochites before Christ in the donor panel also resembles the imperial mosaics of Hagia Sophia where, above the entrance to the nave of the Great Church, an emperor, sometimes identified as Leo VI, kneels before an enthroned Christ. It also occupies an identical position to the Metochites panel. These reflections of the imperial mosaics in Hagia Sophia underscore the pretensions of Theodore Metochites.

Finally, a comparison of the portrait of Isaak Komnenos in the Kariye *Deesis* and the adjacent portrait of Metochites is telling. They bear what we might call a family resemblance. Thus Metochites seems to be inserting himself into the imperial family, becoming heir and descendant of the Sebastokrator Isaak.

The style of the Chora's art and architecture is also instructive. We have seen the mannered style, full of figures with strange postures and different views connected by a decorative veneer; the artful breaking of rules; the extended, evocative narratives; the obscure allusions. Even the marble revetments betray a restless mannerism. In the inner narthex, the patterns consciously avoid the architectural divisions—the framing bands never occur at the pilasters but instead provide a sort of visual counterpoint to the architectural framework. At the edges of the *Deesis* mosaic, the pattern intersects the surface, as if extending beyond it. Such details are odd, to say the least.

What is the connection with Theodore Metochites? Everything, I think, for Metochites was aware of his own originality. Significant parallels to the art of the Chora can be found in Metochites' mannered and self-conscious literary style. His verbose writing is filled with a neo-Homeric vocabulary (frequently of his own invention) along with quotations from the Bible and classical authors, set within an intricate sentence construction that often defies translation. Once, during a struggle for prestige at court, his rival Nikephoros Choumnos began a literary attack, issuing pamphlets in which he accused Metochites of being a repetitious and obscure writer, and a bad astronomer to boot. Metochites countered, ridiculing the "excessive clarity" of Choumnos' literary style, perhaps the greatest insult he could proffer. Certainly neither the art nor the architecture of the Chora could sustain such an accusation.

Like his writings, the complex style of the Chora is an expression of the personality of Metochites the intellectual. The average viewer would have missed the subtleties—they may even have been intended to distinguish the intellectual from the common rabble—and this would have been appreciated by Metochites' coterie of aristocratic intellectuals. Like Post-Modernism, the style of the Chora had snob appeal.

Theodore Metochites was fortunate to find a painter who was, artistically, his equal, and able to respond to the patron's restless intellect and ego. Through careful manipulation of the paintings, he subtly moves the sensitive visitor to honor the benefactor. In the parekklesion, for example, the ideal vantage point for the panoramic sweep of the decoration is directly in front of Metochites' tomb. There the visitor pauses to admire the painting. The gestures and lines of the fresco compositions also lead ultimately to the tomb of Metochites. Similarly, in the inner narthex, the ideal vantage point for the *Deesis* mosaic is on the main axis of the building, directly in front of Metochites' dedicatory portrait. Previous imperial founders may have been honored in the mosaic, and the images of Christ and the Virgin are colossal, but the reverse perspective of the figures places the viewer before the portrait of Theodore Metochites holding the symbol of his achievement. Subtle artistic manipulations, indeed, but ones that doubtless pleased the patron.

Ultimately, despite his ambition and many accomplishments, Metochites proved all too mortal. He was self-centered, anxious, and sensitive. Proud of his hard-won culture and status, which to him were inextricably connected, he was irritated by mediocrity and by the envy of the masses. But human existence was unstable, full of inconsistencies and contradictions. Instability is a recurring theme in Metochites' writings, just as it controls the artistic style of the Chora. In both, compositions seem to unravel and lack focus. Both may reflect the stresses experienced by Metochites and Byzantine society in general during his lifetime.

Metochites' life was in many ways a failure. He was rich, but at the expense of the poor, whom he fleeced as tax collector. He rose high, only to fall dramatically in the palace coup of 1328. Despised by his contemporaries, ousted from office, banished, stripped of his wealth, his palace destroyed, he died a broken man, a simple monk at the monastery he refounded. Nevertheless, as the noted Byzantinist Ihor Ševčenko insists, he deserves our admiration: "To have given us the Chora he had to be a man of wealth, taste, and intelligence. He did not have to be a perfect gentleman."

SELECTED BIBLIOGRAPHY

Major Studies on the Kariye Camii:

E. AKYÜREK, *Bizans'ta Sanat ve Ritüel* (Istanbul, 1996).

Ø. HJORT, "The Sculpture of the Kariye Camii," *Dumbarton Oaks Papers* 33 (1979), 199–289.

R. OUSTERHOUT, *The Architecture of the Kariye Camii in Istanbul*, Dumbarton Oaks Studies 25 (Washington, D.C., 1987).

P.A. UNDERWOOD, *The Kariye Djami*, 3 volumes (New York, 1966).

P.A. UNDERWOOD, ed., *The Kariye Djami*, vol. 4 (Princeton, 1975).

Introduction

S. GERLACH, *Tage-Buch* (Frankfurt, 1674).

R. JANIN, *La géographie ecclsiastique de l'Empire byzantin*, I,iii: *Les églises et les monastères* (2 ed., Paris, 1969), 531–38.

W. MÜLLER WIENER, *Bildlexikon zur Topographie Istanbuls* (Tübingen, 1977).

D. OATES, "A Summary Report on the Excavations of the Byzantine Institute in the Kariye Djami: 1957 and 1958," *Dumbarton Oaks Papers* 14 (1960), 223–31.

A. VAN MILLINGEN, *Byzantine Churches in Constantinople: Their History and Architecture* (London, 1912).

I A First Look

The identification and description of scenes is based primarily on P. A. Underwood, The Kariye Djami, *vol. I.*

O. DEMUS, *Byzantine Mosaic Decoration* (London, 1948).

_____, "The Style of the Kariye Djami and Its Place in the Development of Palaeologan Art," in *The Kariye Djami*, vol. 4, 107–60.

G. ENGBURG, "Aaron and His Sons'—A Prefiguration of the Virgin?" *Dumbarton Oaks Papers* 21 (1967), 279–83.

II A Second Look

The discussion of architecture is based primarily on R. Ousterhout, The Architecture of the Kariye Camii in Istanbul.

S. EYICE, *Son Devir Bizans Mimarisi* (rev. ed., Istanbul, 1980).

C. Mango, *Byzantine Architecture* (New York, 1974).

T.F. MATHEWS, *The Byzantine Churches of Istanbul: A Photographic Survey* (University Park, Penn., 1976).

A.G. PASPATES, *Byzantinai meletai topographikai kai historikai* (Istanbul, 1877), 326–32.

D. PULGHER, *Les anciennes églises Byzantines de Constantinople* (Vienna, 1878), 31–40.

P.A. UNDERWOOD, "The Deisis Mosaic in the Kariye Camii at Istanbul," *Late Classical and Medieval Studies in Honor of A.M. Friend, Jr.*, ed. K. Weitzmann (Princeton, 1955), 254–60.

III A Third Look

This chapter borrows heavily from two articles by R. Ousterhout: "The Virgin of the Chora," in *The Sacred Image East and West*, Illinois Byzantine Studies 4, eds. R. Ousterhout and L. Brubaker (Urbana-Chicago, 1995), 91–109; and "Temporal Structuring in the Chora Parekklesion," *Gesta* 34 (1995), 63–76.

The Akathistos Hymn, ed. E. WELLESZ (Copenhagen, 1957).

AV. CAMERON, "The Virgin's Robe: An Episode in the History of Early Seventh-Century Constantinople," *Byzantion* 49 (1979), 42–56.

A. CUTLER, *Transfigurations: Studies in the Dynamics of Byzantine Iconography* (University Park, Penn., 1975).

O. DEMUS, "The Style of the Kariye Djami and Its Place in the Development of Palaeologan Art," in *The Kariye Djami*, vol. 4, 107–60.

S. DER NERSESSIAN, "The Program and Iconography of the Frescoes of the Parecclesion," in *The Kariye Djami* IV, 305–49.

M.[?] DUCAS, *Historia Turco-Byzantina*, ed. V. Grecu (Bucharest, 1958).

S. EUSTRATIATES, *He Theotokos en te Hymnographia* (Paris, 1930).

J. LAFONTAINE-DOSOGNE, "Iconography of the Cycle of the Infancy of Christ," in *The Kariye Djami*, vol. IV, 195–241.

_____, "Iconography of the Cycle of the Life of the Virgin," in *The Kariye Djami*, vol. 4, 161–94.

H. MAGUIRE, *Art and Eloquence in Byzantium* (Princeton, 1981).

R. OUSTERHOUT, "Collaboration and Innovation in the Arts of Byzantine Constantinople," *Byzantine and Modern Greek Studies* 21 (1997), 93–112.

Service Book of the Holy Orthodox-Catholic Apostolic Church, trans. I. HAPGOOD (New York, 1922).

P.A. UNDERWOOD, "Some Problems in Program and Iconography of Ministry Cycles," in *The Kariye Djami*, vol. 4, 243–302.

N. TETERIATNIKOV, "The Dedication of the Chora Monastery in the Time of Andronikos II Palaiologos," *Byzantion* 64 (1996), 188–207.

IV A Final Look

The life of Theodore Metochites presented here relies on the important paper by I. Ševčenko, "Theodore Metochites, the Chora, and the Intellectual Trends of His Times," *The Kariye Djami*, vol. 4, ed. P. A. Underwood (Princeton, 1975), 17–92.

H.-G. BECK, *Theodoros Metochites: Die Krise des byzantinischen Weltbildes im 14. Jahrhundert* (Munich, 1952).

R. GUILLAND, "Le palais de Thæodore Metochite," *Revue des Études Grecques*, 35 (1922), 82–95.

R. NELSON, "Taxation *with* Representation: Visual Narrative and the Political Field at the Kariye Camii," *Art History*, 22 (1999), 56–82.

_____, "The Chora and the Great Church: Intervisuality in Fourteenth-Century Constantinople," *Byzantine and Modern Greek Studies* 23 (1999), 67–101.

I. Ševčenko, *Études sur la polémique entre Théodore Métochite et Nicéphore Choumnos* (Brussels, 1962).

M. TREU, ed., *Dichtungen des Gross-Logotheten Theodoros Metochites* (Pottsdam, 1895).

GLOSSARY

Akathistos Hymn. A Byzantine hymn to the Virgin, written in the seventh century. It contains an alphabetical list of metaphors for her virginity. According to Byzantine tradition, it was first sung to celebrate the lifting of the Avar siege in AD 626.

Anastasis. The Resurrection. The scene is frequently represented by the Harrowing of Hell, the depiction of Christ's triumph over death through his descent into hell to redeem the souls of the righteous of the Old Testament.

Apse. The semicircular or polygonal recess usually situated at the east end of a church.

Arcosolium. An arched niche containing a tomb.

Barrel vault. A simple semicylindrical vault.

Bema. The sanctuary of a church in which the altar is located.

Blachernitissa. An image of the Virgin, represented with the Christ child in her womb. This image was apparently modelled on a venerated icon housed in the church of the Blachernae at Constantinople.

Deesis. The representation of Christ enthroned between the Virgin and St. John the Baptist, who intercede on behalf of mankind.

Diakonikon. A vestry. By the fourteenth century, the diakonikon at the Chora functioned as a private chapel.

Dodekaorton. The Feast Cycle, representing twelve major scenes from the lives of Christ and the Virgin.

Dogtooth cornice. A projecting horizontal, formed of bricks laid on a diagonal.

Domical vault. A vault constructed above a square or rectangular bay, with a curvilinear surface rising from pendentives at the corners; a sail vault.

Eleousa. An image of the Virgin, known as the Compassionate Virgin.

Esonarthex. The inner entry vestibule (narthex).

Exonarthex. The outer entry vestibule (narthex).

Flying buttress. An exterior arched support, designed to resist the lateral thrust of a building.

Fresco. A method of painting in which pigment is applied to plaster.

Grisaille. A method of painting in grey monochrome, which shows figures and objects in simulated relief.

Groin vault. A vault formed by the intersection of two-barrel vaults, producing a vault composed of four compartments.

Hetoimasia. The prepared throne of "justice and judgment" mentioned in Psalms.

Hodegetria. An image of the Virgin "who shows the way," which is believed to be based on a portrait painted by St. Luke.

Icon. A painting or mosaic of a sacred person, which can be regarded as sacred.

Koimesis. The Dormition of the Virgin; an image of the Virgin lying on a funeral bier.

Ktetor. The founder.

Lunette. A semicircular opening or flat decorative space.

Mandorla. An almond-shaped area of radiant light surrounding a figure.

Mihrab. A niche in a mosque showing the direction of Mecca and hence of prayer.

Mosaic. Decorative work made of small pieces of coloured materials (tesserae) set in plaster.

Naos. The central space for worship in a Byzantine church.

Narthex. An entry vestibule.

Ogival arch. A pointed arch.

Oratory. A place for private worship.

Paleologan art and architecture. The final great revival of the art and architecture of Byzantium, initiated by Emperor Michael VIII Paleologus (1261–82).

Palladium. A holy image to protect a building or city; a safeguard.

Pantokrator. A representation of Christ as ruler of the universe.

Parekklesion. A subsidiary chapel, which is often used for burial.

Pastophoria. The side chapels flanking the bema of a church.

Pendentive. A concave spherical triangle that makes the transition from the square plan of an interior space to the circular plan of the dome that surmounts it.

Prothesis. The chapel where the Eucharist is prepared.

Pumpkin dome. An umbrella dome on a circular base, divided into fluted segments.

Quadrivium. A medieval term for the study of music, geometry, astronomy, and arithmetic.

Revetment. A decorative facing of marble or other material applied to a wall.

Sail vault. A dome-shaped vault that rises directly form the pendentives.

Soffit. The under-surface of an arch or other architectural feature.

Spolia. Reused pieces of stone or carving.

Tessera. A small piece of coloured stone, glass or marble, used in a mosaic.

Theotokos. God-bearer; a title given to the Virgin.

Trivium. A medieval term for the study of logic, rhetoric, and grammar.

Tympanum. An area over a door between the lintel and the arch.

Zoodochos Pege. Life-giving source; a title given to the Virgin.